CURRICULAR CONVERSATIONS

"Margaret Macintyre Latta draws on curriculum theory, philosophy, and the work of artists to develop a wide-ranging notion of play and its place in educational practice. Latta helps readers see what successful teachers, artists, scholars, parents, and others have long known: That play and seriousness walk hand-in-hand in creative human endeavors."

David T. Hansen, Teachers College, Columbia University, USA

"Margaret Macintyre Latta urges us to conceive curriculum as a playful, emergent, and ever-evolving co-creation of meaning and value in a world without start or stop. Thus conceived, each student creates their own circuitous way in awe, wonder, and joy as they move along in the company of teachers, other students, and the whole diverse community including those that only await the call of imagination to join the journey."

Jim Garrison, Virginia Tech, USA

"For Margaret Macintyre Latta, aesthetic play is all about learners being and becoming creators of meaning. In this book, seemingly without effort, she leads us into our potential and the potential of society, to rise above the mis-educative experiences dominating our education today ... and convinces us of the necessity of aesthetic play to awaken the artistic and meaning-making spirit in each of us."

Rita Irwin, University of British Columbia, Canada

"Macintyre Latta offers a model of what the playful engagement with the world that is the center of arts experience can offer to teaching and learning in all disciplines. Featuring a selection of works of art that provide openings to the possibilities of aesthetics and play, Latta's text provides a compelling alternative to impoverished views of education that dominate contemporary calls for educational reform."

Christine Marmé Thompson, The Pennsylvania State University, USA

The central theme of *Curricular Conversations* is this: Play is the thing that brings aesthetic curricular complications near educators and their students, making the lived consequences very vivid, tangible, and possible. Viewing curriculum as genuine inquiry into what is worth knowing, rather than simply a curricular document, this book explores the significances instilled and nurtured through aesthetic play—acting as sustenance for textured curricular conversations, holding catalytic power for investing in lives of passionate engagement with the world, understood as always in the making. Each chapter delves into the space a given artwork reveals. The artworks act as points of departure and/or generative vehicles, foregrounding the roles and possibilities of play within curricular conversations. The translations to the nature of curriculum across disciplines and interests and the lived consequences for learners, learning, and the future are considered, and the reasons to enter into and invest in aesthetic play are explicated. Looking at relevant educational issues, traditions, and theorists through an illuminating lens, this book speaks to curriculum theorists and arts educators everywhere.

Margaret Macintyre Latta is a Professor of Curriculum Theory at The University of British Columbia's Okanagan campus.

Studies in Curriculum Theory

William F. Pinar, Series Editor

For additional information on titles in the Studies in Curriculum Theory series
visit **www.routledge.com/education**

CURRICULAR CONVERSATIONS

Play is the (Missing) Thing

Margaret Macintyre Latta

Routledge
Taylor & Francis Group

NEW YORK AND LONDON

First published 2013
by Routledge
711 Third Avenue, New York, NY 10017

Simultaneously published in the UK
by Routledge
2 Park Square, Milton Park, Abingdon, Oxon OX14 4RN

Routledge is an imprint of the Taylor & Francis Group, an informa business

Library of Congress Cataloging in Publication Data
Macintyre Latta, Margaret, 1955–
Curricular conversations : play is the (missing) thing / Margaret
Macintyre Latta.
    p. cm. – (Studies in curriculum theory series)
    Includes bibliographical references and index.
    1. Curriculum planning. 2. Aesthetics–Study and teaching. 3. Play.
    4. Play. I. Title.
    LB2806.15.M326 2012
    375'.001–dc23   2012029313

ISBN13: 978-0-415-89752-5 (hbk)
ISBN13: 978-0-415-89753-2 (pbk)
ISBN13: 978-0-203-80401-8 (ebk)

Typeset in Bembo
by Wearset Ltd, Boldon, Tyne and Wear

SUSTAINABLE FORESTRY INITIATIVE

Certified Sourcing
www.sfiprogram.org
SFI-01234

Printed and bound in the United States of
America on sustainably sourced paper by
IBT Global

For my parents, Alex and Olive, who always valued play, and my sisters, Patricia and Mary, for their willingness to enter into play.

CONTENTS

ILLUSTRATIONS

PREFACE

To be playful and serious at the same time is possible, and it defines the ideal mental condition. Absence of dogmatism and prejudice, presence of intellectual curiosity and flexibility, are manifest in the free play of the mind upon a topic. To give the mind this free play is not to encourage toying with a subject, but is to be interested in the unfolding of the subject on its own account, apart from its subservience to a preconceived belief or habitual aim. Mental play is open-mindedness, faith in the power of thought to preserve its own integrity without external supports and arbitrary restrictions. Hence free mental play involves seriousness, the earnest following of the development of subject matter. It is incompatible with carelessness or flippancy, for it exacts accurate noting of every result reached in order that every conclusion may be put to further use.

Dewey, 1910, p. 219

This book is invested in making play "wholly play" (Gadamer, 2000, p. 102), disclosing its educative powers and possibilities. To do so, the reader is invited to play as Dewey suggests above, seriously delving into play's curricular presence and potential for all learning. The capacities Dewey notes of *curiosity, flexibility, open-mindedness,* and *earnestness,* insist upon participatory meaning-making, as Gadamer (1986) states, "trying things out." Gadamer explains, "Art begins precisely there, where we are all able to do otherwise" (p. 125). Chapters comprising the book, then, begin with artworks including installations, site-specific art, quilts, film, a physical-media performance, and photography. These artworks prompt reader attention "otherwise," to human capacities for adapting, changing, building, and making meaning and, thus, to the movement of play itself. Play keeps these capacities alive through attending closely to how human beings adapt, build, and make meaning. Gadamer (2000) insists that such play be defined as process, taking place "in-between" self and other(s), drawing attention to the aesthetics of human understanding (p. 109).

Dewey's (1934) *Art As Experience* is American Pragmatism's seminal text on the aesthetics of human understanding. Transcending art objects, Dewey's aesthetics conceives the significance and integrity of all human experience through creating meaning with others and concomitantly creating enlarged understandings of self. This becomes the aim of the book—to put the reader into play with the play of ideas, concretely negotiating meaning-making as a fundamental encounter between self (subject) and other (world). Gadamer (2000) claims play is the clue to ontological explanation (pp. 101–134). Chapters of this book initiate and further this fundamental ontological encounter, putting readers in conversation with artworks alongside theoretical and philosophical perspectives that open into larger curricular conversations.

This book assumes human understanding entails aesthetic play. But, given that both the notion of the *aesthetic* and the notion of *play* have been strangling conceptions historically and personally, the book challenges and reorients these conceptions. The aesthetic is often vaguely associated with the beautiful and sublime and considered to be the exclusive realm of the arts and/or art connoisseur (e.g., Korsmeyer, 1998). The artistic creation becomes the primary object of attention and not the aesthetic experience of creating as intimately connected to its creation. These associations reflect little to no comprehension, and/or rejection, of the Pragmatist tradition (e.g., Granger, 2006; Jackson, 1998; Macintyre Latta, 2001; Waks, 2009). Similarly, play is often solely associated with games and amusements of being a child and extending into adulthood as diversions and forms of relaxation. Play's importance, contexts, and consequences of not playing are documented in the research literature as play deprivation (e.g., Frost, 2010). Play's roles within mental, social, emotional, and physical development are not valued by curricular practices that curtail or entirely eliminate recess, physical education, and the arts from school schedules, never mind eradicating traces of play across the lived curriculum of classrooms and school buildings altogether (e.g., Chappell, 2010; Edwards, Gandini, & Forman, 2011; Meier, Engel, & Taylor, 2010; Paley, 2004; Singer, Michnick, Golinkoff, & Hirsh-Pasek, 2006; Thompson, 2007). In Gadamer's (2000) understandings of play (*spiel*), he foregrounds how play is not an exercise separated from self, but rather reveals its own order and structure to which one surrenders. I know firsthand that the arts can bring the aesthetics of human understanding and play into productive relationship. And, it is this relationship that the book confronts and explores, to find language and practices that free aesthetic play from strangling conceptions, and reveal its cross-disciplinary and inter-disciplinary curricular significances. In doing so, the book characterizes the ways aesthetic play reframes and reorients education, critically providing the sustenance for curricular conversations of all kinds.

So, this book is written primarily for educators from early childhood to adulthood, grappling with their curriculum practices, confined by lack of room to incite and negotiate the movement of play, and grieving the missing substance, connections, relevance, and genuine interest by all involved in relation to the aesthetics of human understandings. Thus, the book is intended to enable educators to build a language for the movement of play and generate images of lived curricular practices that educators will re-envision into their curriculum making, as they seek substance, connections, and relevance, growing interest that furthers and deepens all interests. Specifically, this book addresses arts educators, curriculum theorists, teacher educators, and practicing educators invested in education within the arts, concretely exploring cross-disciplinary and integrated curricular conversations. Additionally, curriculum developers and supervisors, arts advocates, educational administrators, policymakers, parents, and the general community will find important reasons to support and further educators' efforts to do so, world-wide.

The necessity of revealing play's educative character resonated again and again as I turned to particular artists and their artworks. In all cases, I spent time with the artworks that open each chapter and found these works to continue to address me far beyond my initial encounters. As I followed up with associated artists, I found a community that "recognized that our capacity for play is an expression of the highest seriousness" (Gadamer, 1986, p. 130) as these artists enthusiastically embraced the book project. Play and seriousness are deeply interwoven, and although philosophers for centuries have turned to the arts to reveal play's educative character, curricular practices in schools typically still the movement and thwart its powers and possibilities. Nussbaum (2010) explains how "Play teaches people to be capable of living with others without control; it connects the experiences of vulnerability and surprise to curiosity and wonder, rather than to crippling anxiety" (p. 101). Dewey (1934) explains how "art as experience" provides concrete practice with such aesthetics of human understanding. I find the connections to curricular practices to be compelling and it is my hope that readers will seek and build connections too. The language for curricular practices and the lived consequences that the book unfolds are intended to generate the needed terrain for educators and others to claim aesthetic play as integral to the makings of curricula, and seriously invest in these makings as the play currently missing and desperately needed to productively complicate all curricular conversations.

Aesthetic play opens into and cultivates the practice ground to deliberately engage the world. The book traverses this moving terrain, engendering the "worldliness" (Pinar, 2009) to be gained, as play concomitantly engages all involved in confronting the immediacies of the world and envisioning the world being created. Aesthetic play offers the fertile terrain for continuously invigorating all involved within curricular conversations. Thus, the movement of aesthetic play is revealed to be deeply educative, fostering curricular conversations that connect the self and the world in an ever-enlarging conversation.

ACKNOWLEDGMENTS

Many supporters enabled the making of this book, at different phases in its process and in multiple ways. I am indebted to the following people and institutions:

- William F. Pinar, series editor, who saw potential in the makings of this book project from its beginning.
- Naomi Silverman, publisher, Kevin Henderson, editorial assistant, and Amy Vanderzee, marketing assistant, Routledge, who supported the book project across all phases.
- Liora Bresler, Rita Irwin, and Christine M. Thompson, who read and offered reviews during the proposal stages of the project.
- Rita Cihlar Hermann, who provided research assistance throughout the development of the book project.
- The College of Education & Human Sciences at the University of Nebraska-Lincoln, who provided an International Seed Grant that initiated the idea for the book project, and the College of Education and Human Sciences Office of Research, who provided support to complete the project.
- Sharon Kennedy, curator of cultural and civic engagement, and Jorge Daniel Veneciano, director of the Sheldon Museum of Art at the University of Nebraska-Lincoln, whose expertise and insights enabled the development of several chapters in association with exhibits held at the Sheldon Museum of Art.
- Patricia Cox Crews, director, and Carolyn Ducey, curator of collections at the International Quilt Study Center & Museum (IQSCM) at the University of Nebraska-Lincoln, whose expertise and insights enabled the development

of a chapter in association with an exhibit, *Yvonne Wells: Quilted Messages*, curated by Jill Kessler, MA in Textile History/Quilt Studies, University of Nebraska-Lincoln, and co-curated by Jonathan Gregory, IQSCM assistant curator of exhibitions.

- Artists Stephanie Baer, Patricia Cain, Lorraine Cockle, Rondell Crier, Binh Dahn, Jana Napoli, Leighton Pierce, Heather Raikes, and Yvonne Wells, who contributed images of their artworks and so willingly engaged in the project.

- Orville Friesen, Dan Hartig, and Jeff Holland, The Instructional Design Center at the University of Nebraska-Lincoln, whose expertise and artistry enabled the inclusion of images.

- Cindy DeRyke, who greatly assisted with formatting and final editing.

Of course, writing a book about curricular conversations grew out of many substantive conversations with my students (in particular, the doctoral seminar group comprising Teresa Abrahams, Stephanie Baer, Rita Cihlar Hermann, Soon Ye Hwang, Jennifer Nelson, Robert McEntarffer, and Philip M. Ross) and colleagues at the University of Nebraska-Lincoln.

Very importantly, I am grateful for the loving support of my partner, Bill Latta.

My deepest thanks are extended to all.

1

INTRODUCTION

Aesthetic Play Matters to Curricular Conversations

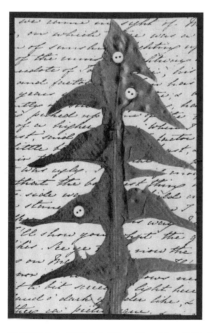

FIGURE 1.1 *I Think That One Day I Shall See ... a Dandelion as a Tree*, Collage/ Ink on Paper, Lorraine Cockle, 2005.

> When the linkage of the self with its world is broken, then also the various ways in which the self interacts with the world cease to have a unitary connection with one another.
>
> *Dewey, 1934, p. 247*

Curriculum as "complicated conversation" (Pinar, 2010) has much to offer to the nature and role of education and the reframing of knowledge. Complicated curricular conversations orient away from commodities to be controlled and inciting competition, toward investments in schools, educators, students, and communities, laboring "to understand themselves and the world they inhabit" (Pinar, 2003, p. 31). This book provides access to educators (and others) to the significance of such curriculum making, attending to the aesthetics of process alongside their students. Therefore, curriculum is understood as genuine inquiry into what is worth knowing, rather than simply a curricular document. It importantly assumes that within the inquiry process lives a worthwhile direction, a medium for teaching and learning that asks teachers and students to participate through adapting, changing, building and creating meaning together. This is the nature of curriculum as aesthetic inquiry. Curriculum is then restored to its etymological roots of *currere* (Pinar, 2009, p. 51), invested in prompting, sustaining, and nurturing a movement of thinking that forms the complicated curricular conversation. Artworks embody this movement through aesthetic play. And, the chapters that comprise this book turn toward artworks to reveal how aesthetic play matters to the formulation of these complicated curricular conversations. It seems there is much to be gained from the elemental nature of play and its aesthetic presence and potential within educative settings across disciplines and interests of all kinds.

As a curriculum theorist, teacher educator, and arts educator, I am concerned that educators world-wide have become weary of cultivating genuine interest in learning, given the lengthy barrage of like-minded global policies and practices concerned predominately with compliance and uniformity (see, for example, Day, 2004; Groundwater-Smith & Mockler, 2009; Kemmis & Smith, 2008; Korthagen, 2001; Loughran, 2006; Smith, 2006; Taubman, 2009). The consequences still the movement of thinking undergirding curricular conversations. Thus, the aesthetic play nurturing and sustaining complicated curricular conversations becomes estranged and foreign. The costly consequences for learners, learning, and the future are apparent as multiplicities are discounted, orienting teaching/learning toward oneness, resulting in generic learning processes and products, and thwarting differences as catalysts in coming to know the self and other(s). Complicated curricular conversations are completely undermined. Increasingly, I am cognizant of how this translates into disinterest on the parts of educators (and their students), unwilling to navigate the given multiplicities and complexities of any educative situation as the aesthetic play integral within all curricular tasks. I encounter educator disinterest as resistance, disregard, distrust, and fear. Dewey (1934) warns, "When the linkage of the self with its world is broken, then also the various ways in which the self interacts with the world cease to have a unitary connection with one another" (p. 247). Dewey identifies how sense, feeling, desire, purpose, knowing, and volition then fall away into separate fragments instilling resistance, disregard, distrust, and fear as ways to exist. His warning is the reality I confront and it does hold frightening significance for teacher education and professional knowledge as teaching is realized as being "severed" from curriculum (Pinar, 2009, p. 11).

This book "intimately" and "necessarily" (Dewey, 1938, p. 20) reconnects teaching and curriculum, providing access to the formative terrain of sensemaking for all educators and students through aesthetic play. It is written for anyone wishing to pursue play seriously in their curricular practices, drawing on aesthetic traditions and engagement, including experimentation, multisensory attentiveness, and non-linear as well as linear ways of thinking and acting. It matters that teachers do not know the formative matters of aesthetic play and thus the complicated curricular conversation is a non-realized possibility. It matters that students do not get to play within complicated curricular conversations, encountering and navigating differences through interaction, deliberation, and debate. This book foregrounds the lived consequences of aesthetic play that are all too often resisted, dismissed, distrusted, and feared by many educators, their students, and others. Each chapter's insistence on complicated curricular conversation as a fully human activity, assuming ways of being in the world that do not separate knowledge from interest, or theory from practice, seeking pervasive qualitative wholes, is intended to confront such stances. And, the book as a whole addresses such resistant, dismissive, distrustful, and fearful stances as constraining and calcifying aesthetic significances for curricular practices and associated understandings of professional knowledge, teacher education, and the nature of learners and learning. Thus, given that the formative nature of all learning seems very unfamiliar, it is curricular terrain more apt to be deliberately avoided by educators. The result is a language of impossibility that quickly consumes and calcifies educators' attempts to aesthetically engage within their curricular practices. These concerns speak directly to the curriculum field because it is the enactment of curriculum that matters (Thornton, 2005).

Finding ways to interrupt the seductive acceptance of what Alexander (1998) terms "maimed versions" of curricular experiences becomes this book's primary task (p. 12). Alexander (2003) explains, "To inhabit the world is not to dominate or renounce it, but to play in it, learn from it, care for it, and realize the beauty of its meanings" (p. 149). Gadamer (2000) insists the reciprocal interactions and modifications entailed within play are fundamental to being human, identifying play as the "clue" to such ontological reciprocity (p. 104). Thus, to learn about other(s) and in turn self, to create and concomitantly be created, is the elemental play ontologically fundamental to being human and integral to the movement of thinking inherent within curriculum as complicated conversation. This book delves into the texture undergirding this clue, exploring how aesthetic play caringly connects self and world and how such reflexive engagement becomes continuous and varied, forming the curricular matter that very much matters.

Philosophers for centuries, from across varied cultures and traditions, have turned to aesthetic experience manifested in and through art forms as means to give expression to and interrogate the play or encounter between self and other (e.g., Bakhtin, 1919; Bourriaud, 1998; Crowther, 1993; Dewey, 1934; Gadamer, 2000; Garrison, 1997; Greene, 1995; Hegel, 1835; Kant, 1790; Merleau-Ponty, 1964; Schiller, 1795; Winston, 2010). The location, purpose, and lived world of the knowing subject are addressed from multiple perspectives, but all value the arts for their capacities to reveal the "in-between" reciprocal space of self and other. Davey (2006) explains how art "works the [in-between] space," stating:

> By bringing to mind what is in effect a transcendent totality of meaning, the artwork reveals … the particularity of its rendition of its subject matter and reveals accordingly that its response is one of many other possible responses. The successful work commands the space that it opens, carefully refining the space between reference and rendition. It is in its ability to disclose and maintain this tension that the dialogical capacity of a work resides.
>
> *p. 63*

Pinar (2011) interprets such in-between spatial workings as providing "passages between subjectivity and sociality" (p. 96) and, thus, acting as points of departure, or as Greene (1995) terms them, "openings" (p. 116). Drawing on these thinkers alongside Davey's (2006) explication that art works this in-between space, this book studies how art does so, residing and inviting us within it, to explore aesthetic engagement, the workings at play. Davey characterizes the understandings evoked as being "unquiet"; that is, understandings that challenge alongside offering opportunities. Contributing chapters embrace aesthetic play as a way to see/act with potential in situations, self, and other(s), entrusting enactment, and navigating unquiet understandings as expected and productive within the workings at play.

Organization of the Book

Dewey (1934), as a Pragmatist, grounds the aesthetic in the art-making experience. In doing so, attention turns to the phenomenology of self–other relations. Such grounding is embodied in the unique human being, located spatially and temporally, and having a particular relationship to all persons, objects, and events in the world. Thus, Dewey's thinking always returns to the activity of the creating individual. It is fitting, then, that a quote from Dewey's scholarship opens each chapter, deliberately selected to invite the reader to play, suggesting conversation among the reader, the imagery, and the associated artist's website, and generating the chapter's continued discussion. Dewey provides key insights and language throughout this book. These insights and language give expression to aesthetic play. Expression is then extended through the thinking of many additional historical and contemporary curriculum theorists, educators, and

philosophers. Readers are expected to join the complicated conversation underway. Chapters can be read separately, but they are intended to fold into each
other and collectively elucidate aesthetic play and its intimate and necessary
connections within curricular conversations.

To concretely map out the terrain of the entire book, the second chapter
experientially unfolds the moving character of aesthetic play. *Begone Dull Care*,
(1949, National Film Board of Canada) a visual/music/animated film directed
by Norman McLaren and Evelyn Lambert in collaborative response with Oscar
Peterson's performed jazz composition, becomes a medium to introduce,
denote, and experience features of aesthetic play. The features encountered
within the film position viewers/readers to enter into play, navigating the
arising complications as interrelated and interdependent contingencies productive within curricular conversations of all kinds. Dull, distanced curricular care
orients very differently than curricular investment of caring matters, intimately
connecting self and world.

Chapters 3 through 9 delve deeper into the texture of aesthetic play, turning
to a cross-section of contemporary art forms to explore ways to see and act with
potential in situations, self and other(s), pursuing curricular implications. These
artworks include installations, site-specific art, quilts, film, a physical-media performance, and photography. Each of these chapters studies the space a given
artwork reveals to me, understanding the arts as "openings" to be experienced
from the "inside" (Greene, 2001, p. 8), and as the generative ground worthy of
inquiry. The artworks act as points of departure and/or catalytic vehicles within
each chapter, surfacing the roles and possibilities of play within curricular conversations. These chapters elucidate how playing brings out the underlying
possibilities of players and the underlying meanings of the world. Such indeter-
minacies ensure the "as if" character that Gadamer (1986) claims is essential to
the nature of play (p. 126). Each artwork offers ways to see "as if," increasingly
understanding seeing as an achievement that is never ending. Akin to the title
and imagery of Figure 1.1, "I think that one day I shall see a dandelion as a
tree,"[1] the permeating task entailed across all chapters asks readers to become a
part of this seeing movement, delving into the "as if" nature of aesthetic play.
Aesthetic play is then experienced as central to curricular practices and meaning-
making of all kinds, and as an investment in the future. As such, aesthetic play
cultivates trust in learning with, from, and through other(s), with participants
coming to see, again and again.

All chapters ask readers/participants to rely on the seeing movement integral
within aesthetic play to incite complicated curricular conversations across disciplines and interests. Specifically, Chapters 3 through 9 navigate particular curricular complications that arise, with each chapter emphasizing an interrelated
and interdependent feature of aesthetic play. But, it is important to keep in
mind that all features form the workings embedded within each artwork and
that the features identified are not finite. A closer look at specific features is

intended to expose the clues, "hidden and withdrawn," that Gadamer (2000, p. 112) refers to within the texture of aesthetic play, revealing curricular possibilities and impacts.

Chapter 3 navigates aesthetic play as elemental to being human. The *Floodwall Project* (2005–2011), a multi-dimensional installation by artist and community activist Jana Napoli with graphic artist Rondell Crier, provides access to the lived consequences of Hurricane Katrina in 2005 in New Orleans, Louisiana, USA. The play of individual curiosities, suggestions, and order-seeking is revealed to hold the vitality, profundity, and continuity for complicated curricular conversations.

Chapter 4 navigates aesthetic play as generative in nature. Site-specific artists' embrace of place calls attention to significances inhering place. UK artist Andy Goldsworthy and the documentary of his site-specific sculptural forms in the making, *Rivers and Tides: Working with Time* (2004, Mediopolis Films), provide insights into valuing the given ground integral to entering into conversation with place and the wisdom harbored within the particulars of place for generating all curricular conversations.

Chapter 5 navigates aesthetic play as needing other(s). Yvonne Wells is an artist/quilt-maker from Tuscaloosa, Alabama, USA. Her quilt exhibit, *Quilted Messages*, (2012, Gottsch Gallery of the International Quilt Studies Center & Museum, University of Nebraska-Lincoln, Lincoln, Nebraska), conveys varied narratives of experience. These quilted messages clothe her reflections, encounters, and stances as she negotiates the materiality of her making processes. The integral role of other(s) within curricular conversations gains visibility, as Wells discloses the concrete realties of her life situated within contextual and historical happenings.

Chapter 6 navigates aesthetic play as embracing the temporal/spatial negotiation of risks and opportunities afforded. The New York-based artist Leighton Pierce uses film, video, and sound to create experiential site-based encounters in time-based media. The unity of space and time is accessed through his installation, *Agency of Time* (2008, Sheldon Museum of Art, University of Nebraska-Lincoln, Lincoln, Nebraska). The agency and belongingness acquired through heightened attention to the abstractions, multiplicities, and uncertainties alive within the present foreground the possibilities and power of space-time at play within curricular conversations.

Chapter 7 navigates aesthetic play as interdependent with imagination, instilling embodied understandings. Heather Raikes is a physical-media artist based in Seattle, Washington, USA. Her (2011) performance artwork, *Corpus Corvus*, is an experimental, integrative telling of the Pacific Northwest Native American myth of the raven. The performance artwork provides access to how sense illuminates understandings, creating room for deliberation, intuition, anticipation, natality, and enlarged realizations. As means of comprehension, embodied imagination reveals the rootedness of all sense-making in the biophysical rhythms of the lived body.

Chapter 8 navigates aesthetic play as demanding attunement to process. Patricia Cain is an artist in Glasgow, Scotland. She collaborates with fellow artists Ann Nisbet, Phil Lavery, Alec Galloway, and Rosalind Lawless to create a multi-media installation, *Drawing (on) Riverside* (2011, Kelvingrove Art Museum, Glasgow, Scotland). The newly constructed Riverside Museum housing Glasgow's transport collection and revealing its maritime history serves as a responsive medium for these artists to consider Glasgow's past, and look to the future, examining the complicities of contexts and peoples. The undertaking entailed collaborators working on-site at the Kelvingrove Museum toward a collective response, continually reconsidered and reformulated through process. The ensuing creative tensions are explored as integral to meaning-making of all kinds.

Chapter 9 navigates aesthetic play as reflexively informing self-understandings in relation to a wider context and citizenry. Binh Danh is a Vietnamese-born photographic artist living in San Jose, California, USA. The images comprising his exhibit, *Viet Nam, Nebraska* (2011–2012, Sheldon Museum of Art, University of Nebraska-Lincoln, Lincoln, Nebraska), convey experiences of the Vietnam War concerned with human memory linked to earth's memory. Dahn's chlorophyll prints, daguerreotypes, and color photography of associated imagery are displayed alongside multi-generational snapshots collected from Vietnamese American families living in Lincoln, Nebraska. The exhibit engages participants in uncovering and re-presenting underlying values, assumptions, and beliefs through expanding personal and collective horizons of knowing. The play of difficulties, distances, and differences that evolves offers much substance for curricular conversations existing between the local and the global, and characterizes a cosmopolitan education.

Throughout the entire book, the nature of curriculum across disciplines and perspectives, and the lived consequences for learners, learning, and the future are considered in relation to the reasons to enter into and invest in aesthetic play. The suggested curricular boldness demands that educators be able to articulate why, how, and what they are orienting their practices toward, and embody these ways of being within their lived practices. Readers are invited to become players in search of language, in search of images of practice. The parts-to-whole relationships moving within and across the book incite play and embody Doll's (2009) depiction of curriculum experienced as *rich, related, recursive,* and *rigorous*. Individually and collectively the chapters will deliberately bring readers near to play's power and potential for rich, related, recursive, and rigorous curricular experiences. Each chapter holds the dwelling space for educators to re-imagine themselves inhabiting their classrooms through investment in play, bringing them near to the particulars of their contexts and relations. Through such "holds upon nearness" (Gadamer, 1986, p. 113) familiarity is gained, and the significances take on lived meanings that are difficult to dismiss. It is such rich, related, recursive, and rigorous holds upon nearness that I see enabling curriculum coming to form as art does, "as a complex mediation and reconstruction of experience" (Pinar, Reynolds, Slattery, & Taubman, 1995, p. 567), translating into curriculums of being in relation, play, care, and beauty, holding significance for teaching and living in the 21st century. These significances suggest greater teacher–student empathy, openness, and appreciation for differences of all kinds, valuing the process character of interaction and deliberation, and translating into greater self-understandings and learning confidence alongside cultivating capacities to live in the world well with others.

Chapter 10 concludes the book, emphasizing how the being of a work of art and its kinship with the nature of play offer much wealth to the inner workings of complicated curricular conversations. Chapter 10 further emphasizes the primacy of significances instilled and nurtured through aesthetic play and the ways they become sustenance for textured curricular conversations. Aesthetic play's catalytic power invests in lives of passionate engagement with the world, understood as always in the making. An immanent and transcendent movement that reconstructs and transforms self manifests the formative terrain worthy of the term education, and its rich, related, recursive, and rigorous complicated curricular conversations.

Play is the Thing, the Persistent Impetus

Shakespeare understood how play could evoke and deepen human understanding, caringly connecting self and world. The telling line adapted for the title of this book is from Shakespeare's *Hamlet*, "The play's the thing, wherein I'll catch the conscience of the King" (1922, Act 2, Scene 2, 603–605), and is embedded within a storied situation to evoke responses from others involved. In the script this line is intended to call into question the conscience of malefactors. Gadamer (2000) terms this "being pulled up short" (p. 268). Kerdeman (2003) unpacks it as the "proclivity for self-questioning and doubt" (p. 294) that I see as catalytic—initiating, sustaining, and nurturing the movement of play itself. Play is the thing, the persistent impetus, calling our very selves into question, and is at the core of complicated curricular conversations. Play is the thing that may bring aesthetic curricular complications near educators, making the lived consequences very vivid, tangible, and possible. Seeing with such active concern is the invitation extended to all who read on. It is a seeing that is multisensory, that Dewey (1934) describes in "The sensible surface of things is never merely a surface" (p. 29). Navigating the sensible texture of aesthetic play forms the terrain of the chapters that follow. As such, readers encounter aesthetic play as Dewey (1934) suggests, through moving "about, within and without, and through repeated visits," letting its structure "gradually yield itself . . . in various lights and in connection with changing moods" (p. 229). Each chapter reveals lights and moods. Artworks illuminate understandings and a language for aesthetic play emerges, prompting prior understandings that reinforce and fold into one another, and contribute to a connected whole. Aesthetic play gains textured understandings through the reader's play with contributing chapters, each offering repeated visits and varying perspectives, seeking what really matters within complicated curricular conversations.

2

"FORCE OF THE POSSIBLE"[2]

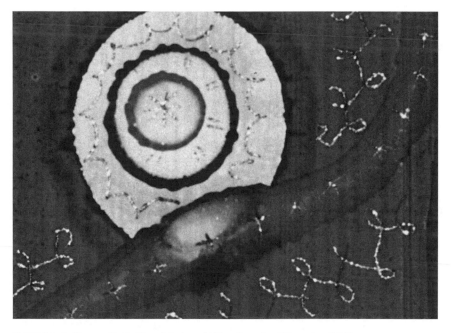

FIGURE 2.1 *Begone Dull Care*, National Film Board of Canada, 1949.

The mental movement must be known before it can be directed.

Dewey, 1904, p. 21

Encountering Dull (Curricular) Care

> Kelly, a student teacher, gathered twenty grade two students closely around her as she introduced and read a story to them. The story held wonderful ideas and her students responded with wonder. But, Kelly did not see or hear the wonder. Instead, she read the story while attending to the clock. In fact, Kelly checked the time, turning her attention entirely away from the children five times, as she read from the story that was relayed in less than five minutes. All efforts on the parts of students to convey their wonder regarding the story were abruptly halted. Students returned to their desks to complete worksheet activities that concerned vocabulary from the story but otherwise seemed quite disconnected from the story itself. Afterwards, as Kelly was asked to reflect about the conduct of her lesson, she was encouraged to return to the story with students the next day to gather and dwell in the wonder a while. She was asked to attend to what her students wanted to share with her about the story. But, Kelly's response was that these were impossible considerations. After all, another story and associated activities were already set for the lesson tomorrow.
>
> *Field Notes, November 17, 2009*

This field text reflects my observations of a student teacher assuming responsibility for a lesson in an elementary classroom in the United States. The observations could be dismissed as a beginning teacher's fumbling navigation of the task of learning to teach. But, worrisome to me as a teacher educator were the surrounding structures and discourses of the school context and personnel, confining and affirming these practices of the student teacher. The necessary lived understandings of curriculum-embracing wonderful ideas were lacking in the experience of the student teacher (and others). Duckworth (2006) calls the "having of wonderful ideas" the "essence of intellectual development" and characterizes teaching as the needed attention to students' wonderful ideas (pp. 1–14). Attending to the wonderful ideas that the story suggested would entail Kelly navigating teaching and learning as concomitantly situated, thoughtful, and intentional. Situatedness entails attending to the particulars of students, contexts, and subject matter. And, although wonderful ideas were tentatively elicited as students listened to the story and examined the accompanying illustrations, Kelly left these ideas masked. Thoughtfulness entails attending to the creation of learning deemed fitting for the given particularities. But, the wonderful ideas deserving to be heard and incorporated into a meaningful learning experience were unaddressed by Kelly. Intentionality entails assuming and seeking relatedness and connectedness among teacher, student, and subject matter. Rather, the wonderful ideas were not enlarged and deepened by Kelly as ways for students to make, relate, and connect their thinking with others.

Feiman-Nemser (2008) insists teaching for wonder integrates "ways of thinking, knowing, feeling and acting into a principled and responsive teaching practice," thus, "complex," "uncertain," and "multidimensional" in nature (p. 699). And, the scholarship on teacher education has for some time revealed that it is within the given complexities, uncertainties, and multiplicities in classrooms that teaching needs to occur (e.g., Cochran-Smith, Feiman-Nemser, McIntyre, & Demers, 2008; Dewey, 1904; Grumet, 2006; Pinar, 2009). This terrain, however, was foreign and feared by Kelly and a dull (curricular) care was all she could muster.

The observation (as recorded) of Kelly's student teaching effort is a salient reminder of the importance of turning attention to the given complexities, uncertainties, and multiplicities of classrooms in the lives of prospective and practicing educators as the necessary "undergoings" and "doings" (Dewey, 1934, p. 44) for occasioning and developing curricular experiences. Situated, thoughtful, and intentional curricular experiences are dynamic and in flux. Curriculum experienced, as such, is always at the nexus of action and place. It is this nexus that forms the undergoings and doings, the wonderings within situations that characterize curriculum. But, as the opening field observation suggests, and Pinar (2009) reaffirms, "emphasis upon evaluation during the last 40 years has led to institutional neglect of the intellectual quality and character of the curriculum" (p. 11). So much so, that Kelly's sense of herself as a teacher is entirely separated from her view of curriculum. She reveals no awareness of curriculum as lived at the nexus of action and place. She has no sense of the necessary discernment demanded of teachers embracing curriculum as "a subjectively animated intellectual engagement with others over specific texts" (Pinar, 2009, p. 11). Moreover, practicing educators reiterate these very concerns, relaying how within their teaching practices they tend to lurch from one decision to the next, rarely asking the epistemological question of what ought to count as knowledge or the ontological question of what teaching for intellectual engagement might feel and look like in practice. Many talk of an awareness of embodied inner tensions, struggling to articulate the underlying reasons, acknowledging that they are dismissing some students, perspectives, differences, and questions. Thus, educators describe a detached teaching identity that becomes an operative mode of address. It is a mode that they do not necessarily feel at ease with, but it becomes a survival mode that entraps them. They further relay how incapacitated they increasingly feel as "fixes" (e.g., national, state-wide, and local standardized educational practices and policies), intended to enhance student achievement alongside teacher and school quality, are mandated and applied. These educational "fixes" are to be carried out by teachers without question, and most often are under-resourced, miscommunicated, and entail little teacher input and/or knowledge about the particular "fix." The research literature reiterates these concerns and documents the ensuing consequences (e.g., Barone, 2001; Block, 2001; Bingham & Sidorkin, 2004;

Cochran-Smith, 2001; Darling-Hammond, 1996; Day, 2000; Groundwater-Smith & Mockler, 2009; Kemmis & Smith, 2008; Nias, 1996; Noddings, 1996). Yet these "fixes" persist. Over and over again the impact of teacher mindfulness concerning the quality and character of the curriculum is vastly underestimated and undermined. The lived consequences for seeing and attending to ethical realms of teaching and learning, to the possibilities of genuine concerted action, to the growth of self-understanding, and to the development of contextually sensitive teaching/learning practices become so limited that I fear a pedagogical blindness subsumes and consumes any sense of wonder about what it means to teach and to learn by all involved.

I seek ways that prospective and practicing teachers might come to see and hear who they are as teachers, so each can see and hear their students and the wonder that is at the core of learning. Seeing and attending to these wonders cultivates complicated conversations that assume the teacher is "a participant in an ongoing multi-referenced conversation" (Pinar, 2009, p. 11) and, as such, inseparable from curriculum as lived. Bal (2002) describes how form, content, and context become interconnected and interrelated, and a "critical intimacy" emerges through the investment of self within such ensuing negotiations. Similarly, Dissanayake (2000) argues that it is human nature to invest in the world, fostering critical intimacy, and that the arts manifest innate human needs to do so through making and elaborating processes (p. 206). This thinking is akin to Dewey (1934), who identifies qualities embodying intimacy such as balance, harmony, rhythm, tension, and form, as "biological commonplaces" to be found in the most elemental human activities (p. 14). Bresler (2004) insists on such involvement as "moving minds," bringing thinking, feeling, seeing, and acting into a vital relationship. All of these interrelated conceptions embrace knowledge as acquired through our being-in-the-world, derived from the act of participation. Epistemology and ontology are thus interwoven on a continual basis. Noddings (1984) turns to the primacy of an ethic of care as the undergirding relational premise. It is care that connects human beings and in turn fosters greater understandings of, and care for, self and other(s). Siegesmund (2010) retraces the thinking of Enlightenment and American Pragmatic philosophers that for centuries have turned to the arts as exemplary forms of such *ontological reciprocity* (Crowther, 1993, p. 2)—the negotiation of self–other relations. Siegesmund, alongside these thinkers, suggests that it is within this space between self and other that learning takes place. I know this to be a vulnerable space; risk and uncertainty abound, but also pleasure and found purpose. It can be uncomfortable, disturbing, and difficult, but also wondrous. The opportunities to experience the qualitative relationships that emerge and to make caring judgments en route offer what Siegesmund conveys as "a curriculum of care and responsible choice" (p. 81). This is the terrain where ethical considerations, possibilities, self-understandings, and contextual considerations are encountered and form and reform complicated curricular conversations. But, as my observation of Kelly's curricular attempt suggests, such relational investment in classrooms is apt to be limited and even denied.

The terrain of complicated curricular conversations is familiar to artists. Attention to the creating process from within the creating process holds significance. The argument has been made repeatedly for aesthetic play's centrality to meaning-making of all kinds (see, for example: Dewey, 1934; Eisner, 2002; Schiller, 1795). An artist brings artworks into existence and the personal interpretive engagement manifests art as always indeterminate. After all, the play brings out the undetermined possibilities of the players and the undetermined meanings in the making. The rootedness of this thinking across time and traditions has been returned to by many interested in revealing the textured terrain encountered through aesthetic play (see, for example: Granger, 2006; Irwin & de Cosson, 2004; Macintyre Latta & Baer, 2010; Waks, 2009). Elucidating how art works this terrain discloses the workings of human experience alongside the developing process of self-formation. Such relational investment is what curriculum as complicated conversation envisions education ought to entail. But, the nature of this play that is not instrumental or applied needs to be practiced. Its features, enabling deliberate and responsible engagement without knowing exactly what is going to come of it, must gain greater physicality and materiality. Aesthetic play's interdependency with curriculum-making must be concretely experienced. The title of an artwork, *Begone Dull Care* (1949), a visual/music/animated film directed by Norman McLaren and Evelyn Lambert in collaborative response with Oscar Peterson's performed jazz composition, draws my attention. As I attend to the film, I find that it provides the terrain for readers to enter into play; residing and inviting viewers within the space it creates, to experience the ground-disclosing aesthetic play and awakening care.

Entering Into Play: Navigating the Complications

The experimental film *Begone Dull Care* (1949) chronicles McLaren's and Lambert's aesthetic play of scratching and painting on the emulsion of the filmstrip itself as they attend to Peterson's jazz composition. It is documented as a collaborative undertaking (Richard, 1982), with participants seeking ways "of being dialogical in relation" to the text engaged together (Greene, 1995, p. 116). As viewers attend to the film, the qualitative relationships emerging and the judgments navigated in process are concretely experienced. The act of creating meaning entails participants investing and elaborating within the constraints and affordances of these qualities and ensuing judgments (Eisner, 2002, pp. 236–238). The morphing imagery moves fittingly with the music in a vertical stream, becoming a living shape (see: www.nfb.ca/film/begone_dull_care_caprice_couleurs). Schiller (1795) explains that "only as the form of something lives in our sensation, and its life takes form in our understandings, is it living shape" (p. 76). The film provides access to just such an experience, acting as a "force of the possible" (Baldacchino, 2009, p. 58). The content and form of the film are inextricably linked, taking life shaped through the "relationality" (Biesta, 2004) present and manifesting. Aesthetic play as a way to see and act with potential in situations, self, and other(s) positions all players to navigate the relational complexities as elemental to being human, generative in nature, in need of the other, embracing the temporal/spatial negotiation of risks and opportunities afforded, interdependent with imagination, instilling embodied understandings, demanding attunement to process, and reflexively informing self-understandings in relation to the wider context and citizenry. I bring my voice and experiences to bear as I navigate these complications attending to the film, and invite readers/viewers to do so too, cultivating curricular possibilities.

Elemental to Being Human

Interactive engagement is how human beings interpret and make sense of their worlds from birth, and, some argue, from beginnings in the womb (see, for example: Dewey, 1934; Dissanayaki, 2000; Grumet, 1988; Johnson, 2007; Noddings, 1984). Following the moving text of the film invites my engagement. The shapes of previous encounters are recalled as the film is shaped. The confluence of imagery and music regenerate and redirect expectations. Gadamer's (2000) description of foregrounding seems fitting, stating, "Whatever is being foregrounded must be foregrounded from something else, which in turn, must be foregrounded from it" (p. 305). Gadamer explains that the process nature of foregrounding brings prejudices into play, acknowledging the specifically situated and historically conditioned nature of all understanding. Situating myself within the historical, social, political, and cultural traditions and contexts influencing and interacting with given experiences is the unfinished creative task elemental to being human, to living itself.

Generative by Nature

The living shape the film takes is the generative terrain of creating meaning. The relationships among thinking and the materials, sounds, expressions, and movements encountered and negotiated by the artists, McLaren, Lambert, and Peterson (1949), are made visible and tangible. I engage similarly. Entering as a creator into such a living shape assumes participatory engagement through making and relating, perceiving and responding, and connecting and understanding. It is these artistic thinking processes that suggest and open paths to follow and navigate for all involved (Macintyre Latta & Chan, 2011). The multisensory engagement necessitated through attending to sensory qualities and relations is the work of perception, actively shaping the act of responding. The discursive movement prompted demands alertness and openness to the possibilities that present themselves. The creative terrain forms through responsiveness to the features encountered and the relations that transpire. Berger (1972) explains it this way: "The relation between what we see and what we know is never settled" (p. 7). The negotiating room in-between allows for thinking and feeling through wondering, questioning, analyzing, and reconsidering, manifesting the responsive creation or invention of meaning. Awareness of the purposeful construction of such meaning enables the search for and articulation of personal connections. The generative nature of aesthetic play assumes such a mindful trust in process, embracing the contingencies and the significances as the meanings to be found and made there.

In Need of the Other

The film invites me to venture forth, seeking personal relations and responses. Dewey (1934) explains it this way:

> To perceive, a beholder must create his [sic] own experience. And his [sic] creation must include relations comparable to those which the original producer underwent.... Without an act of recreation the object is not perceived as a work of art.
>
> *p. 54*

In other words, the act of recreation necessitated here is comprehensively participatory thinking, creating meaning with others and concomitantly creating enlarged understandings of self. The ongoing reflexivity between self and other is the task assumed. The movement shaped and reshaped as the film unfolds, continually positions otherness as an operative construct to negotiate. It is the other that calls my making and relating, perceiving and responding, and connecting and understanding into question. It is the other that asks me to see/hear/feel/touch within specific moments. It is the other that incites a turn and return to self-understandings. The moving motifs in accord with the music reveal the ensuing multisensory self–other negotiation. Bowman (2004) explains, "Knowing is doing and always bears the body's imprint" (p. 46). The moving motifs form the imprints navigated across self and other, with knowing understood to be in need of the other and inseparable from response/action.

Embracing the Temporal/Spatial Negotiation of Risks and Opportunities

The ongoing movement of the film positions the givens of present moments to be encountered and negotiated continuously. Dewey (1934) explains that separating the spatial from the temporal is destructive to this process character, foregrounding how the spatial and temporal must operate together (pp. 183–184). Space and time, rather than being bound commodities, are experienced as reciprocal, in flux, and situated. Therefore, the past can be traced within the present and the future can be anticipated. The temporality alive within the present demands a mindfulness of the communicative, relational, and interactive practices that ensue within the givens of space. These practices hold the contingencies that must be embraced as the risks and opportunities to be worked with as productive. Process must be valued through the discord, disturbance, and disequilibrium encountered, as well as the accord, unity, and harmony to be found and navigated within attention to the movement. This is what Dewey (1938) called "social control," with the control coming from within the situation itself rather than being imposed from outside or predetermined (pp. 51–60). Attention to Dewey's (1938) translation of such control as an "ever-present"(ing) process assumes the forming and reforming ground of meaning-making is always shifting (p. 50), suggesting future directions that are not predetermined.

Interdependent with Imagination, Instilling Embodied Understandings

The film demands the work of imagination, actively soliciting and engaging my ideas in particular images and sounds. The expression gained arises out of the opportunities afforded by wandering, interacting, deliberating, and re-imagining throughout. It is a participatory experience. It entails connecting my past to the ideas encountered, which Dewey (1934) depicts as the conscious adjustment of new and old understandings through surrender and reflection (p. 53). Thus, Dewey identifies imagination as "the only gateway through which these meanings can find their way into present interaction" (p. 276). Imagination as the gateway insists that it is not understood as a distinct specialized faculty of the mind, but a capacity to see with potential in situations, self, and other(s). Greene (2001) explains that "What the arts offer us, then, is the releasing of our imagination, enabling us to move into the as-if—to move beyond the actual into invested worlds, to do so within our experience" (p. 82). And, as Granger (2003) further explains, imagination entails "the active reconstructive project itself" (p. 54). The film engages my imagination likewise. The work of art that the film shapes is the product of such imaginative releasing and reconstruction. Viewers that engage the task similarly will find their own reconstruction, interdependent with the interactions and involvement evoked through the elemental role of the body. Dewey refers to such multiple sensory engagements as the biophysical rhythm of the lived body (pp. 162–186). One's thinking, feeling, seeing, and acting is brought into relationship with the complexities encountered. Each brings forth characteristics of the other. Merleau-Ponty (1962) refers to this as a fundamental reversibility experienced through one's body, "the fabric, into which all objects are woven, and it is, at least in relation to the perceived word, the general instrument of my comprehension" (p. 235). The embodied impacts "translate" the senses into each other (p. 235), belonging as much to the other as self. Thus, the film cannot be separated from the acts that made it so, with the embodied impacts forming the sensible ground occupied with instilling connections.

Demanding Attunement to Process

I experience the music and imagery evolving organically throughout the film. The music and imagery are not simply matters to be continually reckoned, but rather the matter that suggests patterns and structures forming a rhythmic movement. It is a movement that shapes an organic whole. And, it is a movement that manifests the vitality of all relations present and ongoing. Three interrelated and interdependent segments take shape and give structure to the rhythmic moving form. The first segment associates imagery with specific instruments in sync. For example, the sounds of the bass merge with red imagery and the sounds of the piano merge with vertical and horizontal lines. But the qualities, relations, and connections that ensue quickly complicate the perceiving and receiving of movement. Such complications fold into the second segment, delving into the texture I now see and feel. The slowed movement creates space and time to concretely experience the physicality and materiality of the found ordered development. It is this dynamic ordered character of the work that leads to the third and final segment that picks up considerable momentum. The thoughtful, careful negotiation of the second segment becomes less controlled in the third segment, seeking more spontaneity without losing unity. It is unity that achieves order across the three segments. It is unity that engages all involved in a continued search for attunement. It is unity that is the attunement that constitutes art. Dewey (1906) explains: "To feel the meaning of what one is doing, and to rejoice in that meaning; to unite in one concurrent fact the unfolding of the inner life and the ordered development of material conditions—that is art" (p. 292).

Reflexively Informing Self-understandings

The rhythmic movement of the film is marked by emphases and patterns. Repetition is encouraged as ideas and practices are revisited. But, given the animated circumstances, repetition is a recursive movement that is not in any way static. Rather, it is dynamic, with the recursive movement unfolding as a continuous process of coming to see; a backward movement that re-covers and re-presents alongside a forward movement that generates and evokes new thinking. Dewey (1934) calls the ensuing rhythm "esthetic recurrence"— relationships that sum up and carry forward (p. 166). These recurrences present themselves in different contexts and with differing consequences so that every recurrence is "novel as well as a reminder" (p. 169). Locating self within this movement is thus ongoing, as relations are encountered again and again. Renewal of self-understandings is reflexively fostered throughout, as new perspectives are encountered and navigated in relation to the wider context. O'Loughlin (2006) explains that "from this kind of relation, individuals gain and generate kinds of lived knowledge in contrast to that sort of knowledge which is excessively abstract and removed from actual practice" (p. 155). Here, context is importantly experienced as derived through concrete connectedness with other(s). O'Loughlin explains how seeking such curricular connections with others cultivates "citizenry" and insists it must be practiced (pp. 149–168). In doing so, Hansen (2011) argues, conceptions of self "in and for the world" enlarge and deepen, constituting the journeying of a cosmopolitan education (p. 46).

Begone Dull (Curricular) Care

It seems aesthetic play is experienced at the nexus of situation and interaction; thus, it is living inquiry that is attentive to the givens of context, the particulars involved, and the relational complexities that ensue. The structure of aesthetic play is dependent on the play itself, resisting means and ends, reliant on the performance (Gadamer, 2000, p. 134). By aesthetic play's very nature, dialogue, interpretation, and interaction are expected. A structure is generated through play that offers directions for proceeding. Gadamer reminds us of this, stating that play has a spirit of its own that must be attended to and embraced. He calls it "transformation into structure" (p. 110). The structure forms as the nature of aesthetic play is concretely experienced, asking participants to enter into the play as elemental to being human, generative, creating meaning, cognizant of needing other(s), embracing the temporality and spatiality of any given moment, releasing and reconstructing meaning through imaginative and embodied engagement, pursuing attunement, and reflexively situating and renewing self-understandings. Gallagher (1992), unpacking Gadamer's thinking, conveys how such play entails a movement of *appropriation* and *transcendence*. Gallagher is careful to emphasize that it is the movement encompassing both appropriation and transcendence that constitutes the dynamic structure (p. 49). Play is the thing, the movement that evokes lostness to the play itself, transcending self and other. Gadamer (2000) states "Play fulfills its purpose only if the player loses himself [sic] in play" (p. 102). And, play evokes foundness through appropriated self-understandings. Play is therefore the work of self-growth more than self-realization. There is an investment of self that Gadamer portrays as

> the player . . . never simply swept away into a strange world of magic, of intoxication, of dream; rather it is always his [sic] own world, and he [sic] comes to belong to it more fully by recognizing himself more profoundly in it.
>
> *pp. 133–134*

The belongingness cultivates caring through play, experienced as "intimately" and "necessarily" (Dewey, 1938, p. 20) tied to its enactment. It is not a dull, distanced care but rather a personally invested caring that grows through inner necessities and not externally imposed reasons. A felt freedom emerges that fosters a spirit of inquiry, making room for wondering, reconsidering, and speculating. The possibilities arising out of care are what generates and directs the movement. If care is non-existent or thwarted, any movement is stilled or constrained. Dewey (1934) warns that sense, feeling, desire, purpose, knowing, and volition then fall away into separate fragments, instilling resistance, disregard, distrust, and fear as ways to exist (p. 247). Aesthetic play caringly connects self and world and such reflexive engagement becomes continuous and varied.

It is play's complications that enable curriculum to come to form "as a complex mediation and reconstruction of experience" (Pinar, Reynolds, Slattery, & Taubman, 1995, p. 567), translating into textured curricular conversations of being in relation, play, care, and beauty, holding significances for teaching and living in the 21st century. But play's catalytic nature within curriculum across disciplines and interests, and the lived consequences for learners, learning, and the future, are rarely glimpsed and/or felt. Educator resistance, disregard, distrust, and fear of such teaching experiences reflects how play's mindful trust in process, embracing the contingencies and the significances as the meanings to be found and made, are more apt to be unknown. Dewey (1904) states:

> To recognize the signs of its [mental play] presence or absence, to know how it is initiated and maintained, how to test it by results attained, and to test apparent results by it, is the supreme mark and criterion of a teacher. It means insights into soul-action, ability to discriminate the genuine from the sham, and capacity to further one and discourage the other.
>
> *p. 14*

Dewey further emphasizes that "the mental movement must be known before it can be directed" (p. 21). It matters that teachers do not know the formative matters of play and thus the complicated curricular conversation is a non-realized possibility. It matters that students do not get to play within complicated curricular conversations, encountering and navigating differences through interaction, deliberation, and debate. Perhaps these matters form the reconstructive cosmopolitan curriculum project desperately needed.

The play undergirding curriculum as complicated conversation brings participants near to the ethics and complexities that come with being in relation within specific situations with other(s). It is a nearness that positions participants to attend to the particular contexts and relations. It is a nearness that positions participants to continually seek connections with surroundings. The complicated curricular conversations that ensue "encourage students to reconstruct their own lived worlds through their reanimation of the material they study" (Pinar, 2010, p. 5), thus translating into curriculums of being in relation and caring. Play is the thing, forming through its insistence on contingencies, and generating pedagogical significances with lasting value, a body–world relationship. This dynamic interchange of aesthetic play is the lived conjuncture of body–world that confronts the immediacies of the world we live in and envisions the world we are creating together. The bold entry into these conversations demands a wakefulness that belongs as much to the other as to the self. Such wakefulness holds the curricular presence and potential inherent within play. Aesthetic play is a medium. The interplay discloses understandings alive within the movement itself. And the movement must play on in our *pedagogical imaginaries*. "This is where the imagination is not just a matter of individual cognition but an activity of the mind that empowers us to engage with its larger context—that of the imaginary" (Baldacchino, 2009, p. 128). The art of complicated curricular conversations brings forth these possibilities through play.

The possibilities at play in complicated curricular conversations are the children's wonderful ideas that were held at bay by the student teacher in the opening field note. Duckworth (2006) is clear that:

> Intelligence cannot develop without matter to think about. Making new connections depends on knowing enough about something in the first place to provide a basis for thinking of other things to do—of other questions to ask—that demand more complex connections in order to make sense. The more ideas about something people already have at their disposal, the more new ideas occur and the more they can coordinate to build still more complicated schemes.
>
> *p. 14*

The possibilities of play enliven teaching and learning and hold significances that foster purposes and strengths in all involved. Pursuing these purposes and strengths is the "force of the possible" that the teaching body must embody. Education must cultivate the conditions to do so for its "release" (Greene, 1995). All children deserve teachers that will invest in such complicated curricular conversations.

3

ELEMENTAL TO BEING HUMAN

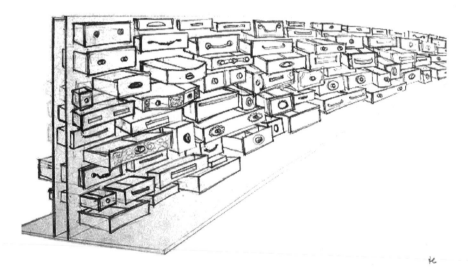

FIGURE 3.1 *Floodwall Sketch, Original Wall Configuration*, Rondell Crier, 2005.

> One can teach others to think only in the sense of appealing to and fostering powers already active in them.
>
> *Dewey, 1910, p. 30*

Artist and community activist Jana Napoli describes how she returned to her home in New Orleans, Louisiana, USA, following the devastating floodwaters of hurricane Katrina in 2005. Napoli's response to the overwhelming devastation became an installation project titled *Floodwall* (2005–2011), relaying the silence she experienced as surrounding and troubling her return. She further describes how the permeating silence was so very unexpected. At a distance, the televised imagery and news reports did not convey the devastation's deeply personal, concretely experienced presence or weight. Napoli found herself wading into the engulfing silence, "instinctively" seeking meaning of some kind (www.floodwall. org). The nature and shape of such meaning-making became the Floodwall Project, a multi-dimensional artistic installation created with graphic artist Rondell Crier. Napoli created an installation using retrieved dresser drawers as building bricks that sometimes form a wall measuring 8 feet tall and 192 feet in length, and at other times fall in disarray across the floor, and can be configured into a room. Crier created an interactive database, documenting as much information as could be ascertained through numbering, cataloguing, and photographing each drawer. Additionally, audio and video components include a growing collection of oral histories from the original drawer owners. The associated website brings those interested near to experiencing this artistic installation through images, artists' statements, personal narratives, news reports, audio/video recordings, curriculum guides, and additional resources. As a whole, it is a work of art brought into existence by Napoli and Crier to make sense of a significant human experience.

The Floodwall Project and the associated website provide important access to the lived consequences of the hurricane through tracing what the silence held for Napoli and Crier, and prompts in others. Common elemental responses are elicited as the overwhelming sense of loss, alongside the human capacity to seek meaning, and are conveyed through multiple lenses. Dewey (1910) describes this human capacity for meaning-making to be embedded within innate resources as "the powers already active" in self and others. He identifies *curiosity, suggestion,* and *orderliness* as powerful resources fundamental to human beings (p. 30). As I trace the creation of the Floodwall Project via the website, the sudden individual and collective discord is first expressed and experienced, but reflection is also induced. The natural resources of curiosity, suggestion, and orderliness become tangible through the experiences of others and are awakened in me. This chapter examines these resources and their active nature within learning of all kinds.

The Vitality of Curiosity

Napoli (2005) finds herself called to engage the silence she feels, sees, hears, and touches upon returning to her New Orleans home after the retreat of the floodwaters, despite the hugely difficult circumstances and personally distressing time. The multisensory engagement with place and the ensuing displacement evokes a physical need to observe, gather, and reflect. It is within physiological unease that

Dewey (1910) claims curiosity manifests (p. 31). Napoli describes how she observed the pieces of people's lives scattered all over neighborhoods and how she felt compelled to gather and reflect on the tales each piece might tell. As Napoli wandered the streets, she began to collect drawers from dressers, kitchen cabinets, desks and bureaus, "empty of their contents but suffused with memories" (www. floodwall.org). She collected 710 drawers in all. Yet, as Dewey states:

> there is more than a desire to accumulate just information or heap up disconnected items.... In the feeling, however dim, that the facts which directly meet the senses are not the whole story, that there is more behind them and more to come from them, lies the germ of intellectual curiosity.
>
> *p. 32*

Dewey (1910) identifies curiosity as the vitality within engagement of all kinds (p. 30). And, akin to Napoli, as I enter the Floodwall Project website, my observations, gathering, and reflecting germinate vitality, "yielding new qualities" (Dewey, 1910, p. 32). Social interaction and engagement instill "eagerness for a larger acquaintance with the mysterious world in which [s]he is placed" (p. 32). Such eagerness finds its own compelling intellectual path. Napoli allowed each of the drawers she gathered to speak to her. She found herself wondering what each drawer revealed about the lives they were previously connected to; how each drawer might reflect the fate of the original owner; and, in what ways the drawers could be arranged and rearranged to bring others close to the loss of lives, homes, and sense of/and need for place. Indeed, the Floodwall website brings me near to these wonderings too. Curiosity is germinating. I attend to the imagery on the website and am intrigued by the individual character of each drawer and the world each might recall. Napoli's artist statement (see www.floodwall.org) allows me to imagine her walking through her devastated community, and to trace the beginnings of this project. I find myself feeling connected to Napoli's experience and I explore the website further. I think of the junk drawer in my kitchen and the collection of artifacts it holds that tell many tales of family, friends, and events that form the "stuff" of my life. I look at the site for evidence of a similar junk drawer. I read the continuous cycle of narrative excerpts from drawer owners accounting for the lost contents. I listen to the audio recordings from identified owners. I hear about the artifacts each of their drawers held. The weighted emptiness all drawers now hold envelops me as I navigate the site, finding my way through the installation configurations, database, and visual/audio recordings.

The Profundity of Suggestion

Qualities arise that elicit my genuine interest, as I navigate about and through the website. I seek more information about hurricanes in general and Katrina in particular. I desire to know more about New Orleans and its people, including its history, culture, climate, topography, resources, and economy. Questions come to my mind that I did not have before I entered the website. I confront the fact that one million Gulf Coast residents suddenly became homeless. I realize that Hurricane Katrina triggered the largest housing crisis in American history since the Great Depression. The extent of poverty becomes increasingly visible to me as the lives are collectively storied. My ignorance and complicity are directly exposed. Personal values, assumptions, and beliefs are reevaluated as matters of privilege are seen in new ways, challenging my blindness to others. Issues of race and class, and the divides between the Third World and the American Dream become much more complex in nature.

Dewey (1910) describes the functional dimensions of such suggestive powers to have an *ease, range,* and *depth* (pp. 34–37). Ease is derived through genuine participation in sense-making entailing a thinking movement of surrender and reflection (Dewey, 1934, pp. 53–54). It is through my surrender to the experiences afforded by the Floodwall Project that suggestive ease is enabled. Thus, it is an ease that assumes a reciprocal relationship, revealed as interaction and deliberation, putting me in an ongoing reflective conversation with the project. Openness, alongside belief in process, is demanded of me through seeing and acting as situations call forth. Relations emerge, presenting themselves as a range of invitations for possible exploration. And, as Dewey (1910) emphasizes, "Thinking is specific, in that different things suggest their own appropriate meanings, tell their own unique stories, and in that they do this in very different ways with different persons" (p. 39). The Floodwater Project creates such a space for me to enter and experience the complexity of subject matter with ease, range, and depth. It is a space that necessarily works with time to foster the profundity of "what is not yet given" (Dewey, 1910, p. 34). Yet, it is within the given particularities of the project, and my experiences brought to bear, that ease, range, and depth give shape to the inquiry path I find myself taking.

The Continuity Achieved Through Seeking Order

Dewey (1910) explains that "thinking is not like a sausage machine which reduces all materials indifferently to one marketable commodity, but is a power of following up and linking together the specific suggestions that specific things arouse" (p. 39). It is this movement of thinking, entailing *following up* and *linking together,* that achieves order. Continuity is instilled through deliberate efforts over time. Throughout my exploration of the Floodwall Project, I keep returning to a press release the National Law Center for Homelessness and Poverty (2005) made, drawing attention to how Katrina made homelessness a more familiar concept. The familiarity gains concrete expression through the artifacts, personal accounts and images, voice intonations, and installation configurations. The accounts of secondary displacement due to hurricane Katrina shared by former residents of New Orleans on the website of the Floodwall Project describe how each confronted the immediacies of new places and attempted to negotiate new lives. Aspects of these accounts resonate and bring connections to my mind. As Dewey (1910) explains, it is this following up and linking movement in which "All kinds of varied and incompatible suggestions may sprout and be followed in their growth, and yet thinking be consistent and orderly, provided each one of the suggestions is viewed in relation to the main topic" (p. 40).

Order is therefore dynamic. The Floodwall Project reflects such ordering. Time and growth are embraced as interrelated features that instill this ordered dynamic. Dewey (1934) identifies how *time* and *growth* infused with *inception*, *development*, and *fulfillment* (p. 55) fold into every part of the experiential whole. The form of the whole is therefore present in every part—the artifacts, personal accounts and images, voice intonations, and installation configurations of the Floodwall Project. Each part offers moments of synthesis and carries forward into new relations for the artists involved. The opportunities for myself (and others) to retrace and experience this parts-to-whole movement incites new and enlarged understandings of homelessness as the relations layer into each other. The understandings gained by all involved arise out of the opportunities afforded and taken, generated out of the particular interactions and involvement incited. Napoli's work of art is recreated in the experience of each viewer/participant. These experiences will differ, but it is the ongoing search for continuity that the Floodwall Project positions everyone entering it to embrace and organize, "bringing to living consciousness an experience that is unified and total" (Dewey, 1934, p. 15).

Locating the Problem of Education

The Floodwall Project draws attention to a devastating experience and how, no matter what, human beings are compelled to seek meaning as they live their lives. The installation is described on the website as a "floodwall against the erasure of the ordinary people and the everyday rhythms of life from which great cities are formed" (www.floodwall.org). It is important to emphasize that this meaning was arrived at as the artists and all involved had time and space to make sense of the significant experience. In fact, the meaning gains much depth and breadth because of the personal attention to the process of meaning-making throughout. All moments found en route offer sense-making integration and synthesis, layer into each other, and form a textured fullness that gives substance to the significances of the Floodwall. The Floodwall Project voices how integral the freedom to actively participate in the making of knowledge is and creates a space for others to find their voices and make meanings. And, in doing so, the Floodwall Project points to the consequences of abandoning active meaning-making.

Of course, meaning as primary to living and learning is not a new concern. Education scholars for some time have argued for learning spaces occasioning mcaning–making opportunities (see, for example, Bruner, 1990; Dewey, 1916; Hostetler, 2011; Hostetler, Macintyre Latta, & Sarroub, 2007; Noddings, 1993; Schwab, 1976), encountering affections and aversions. Dewey (1916) insists that it is within *affections* and *aversions* that meaning is made (p. 188). He clarifies that "such knowledge never can be learned by itself; it is not information, but a mode of intellectual practice, a habitual disposition of mind" (p. 188). But Dewey (1910) locates the problem of education in the lack of regard for the mode of meaning-making, valuing the presence and power of human beings' natural resources of curiosity, suggestion, and order as habitual dispositions within learning of all kinds (p. 44).

What is too often misunderstood is that it is not the curricular activities themselves that occasion these meaning-making opportunities and powers. Curricular activities must actively create room for students' curiosity, suggestions, and ordering, and foster their incorporation and development as resources for inquiry. The teachers' roles and associated responsibilities to do so within the selection, preparation for, and enactment of curricular activities are pivotal. As a teacher, I have felt the lure to disregard these elemental human resources and instead trap knowledge into palatable pieces for student digestion. This lure's seduction lies in the ease established and sustained by negating the presence of any complexities within learning contexts. Such negation dismisses complexities in students, teachers, and contexts, assuming a generic sameness. But I have also felt the lure of attending to complexities in my teaching practices. A compelling movement ensues, that is transformative for all. In resisting the compulsion to halt and control, I allow the moment to unfold, accepting its challenges and shifts. Completely immersing myself in the teaching/learning moment and then releasing the moment demands an elemental response. My curiosities are called upon. "When," "why," "how," and "what" I know within such teaching/ learning situations is always contingent, suggesting an organizing dynamic all its own. Inhering in this undertaking asks teachers and students to invest in what is particular and irreplaceable in each curricular situation. Such invested curricular situations are infused with emotional commitment in which learning is not simply an object nor a concept, but a feeling or attitude that insists on one's interest and participation.

The Floodwall Project website chronicles the artists' participatory thinking through the relations and connections made (see www.floodwall.org). As I explore the site, the relations and connections I see and make affirm and foster my continued participatory thinking. Bakhtin (1919) characterizes participatory thinking as entering into a relationship with content that fosters an "emotional volitional tone circumfusing the whole" (pp. 33–34). He clarifies:

> That content, after all, does not fall into my head like a meteor from another world, continuing to exist there as a self-enclosed and impervious fragment, as something that is not woven into the unitary fabric of my

emotional-volitional, my living and effective, thinking-experiencing, in the capacity of an essential moment in that thinking-experiencing.

p. 33

It is the relations that offer paths for interaction and deliberation. It is the relations that create a parts-to-whole meaning-making process. It is the relations that cultivate axiological stances throughout. It is the relations that cultivate belongingness. Dewey (1934) clarifies that this is not a cause-and-effect understanding of relation, but rather about "generation, influence, and mutual modification" (p. 134). It is within this moving and changing experience that emotion manifests as a permeating, palatable, invigorating energy. Dewey (1934) similarly states:

> Emotion is the moving and cementing force. It selects what is congruous and dyes what is selected with its color, thereby giving qualitative unity to materials externally disparate and dissimilar. It thus provides unity in and through the varied parts of an experience.
>
> *p. 42*

The Floodwall Project's varied parts work together, orienting sense-making through curiosity, suggestion, and orderliness for anyone that enters into relationship with its content, creating her/his own meaning-making rhythm and intonation. A temporal ordering evolves with a unique pace and associated emphases found en route. So, the meanings I make are distinct from others', but as Bakhtin (1993) states, it is "the experience of an experience as *mine*" (p. 36). The intimate emotional connectedness of such an experience is understood by Dewey (1934) as being instilled, working with time. He turns to the illustrative examples of watching a dramatic play on a stage or reading a novel to explicate his thinking, stating, "it attends the development of a plot; and a plot requires a stage, a space wherein to develop and time in which to unfold. Experience is emotional but there are no separate things called emotion in it" (p. 42). The Floodwall Project reveals such a plot design, providing an unfolding space for sense-making that invites curiosity, suggestions, and orderliness. Emotions are attached to the concrete investment and concern is elicited through engagement and enactment.

Bakhtin (1993) identifies a principle "my non-alibi in Being" that reaffirms to me that ignoring the role and place of self-investment within living and learning produces passivity, resulting in abdication and indifference (p. 42). Bakhtin explains that living in a world where all content is imposed would be untenable. He states that "in that world I am unnecessary, I am essentially and fundamentally non-existent in it" (p. 9). There is a deep kinship here with Dewey's (1934) notion of the "live creature": in continuous interaction with the environment through adapting, changing, building, and making meaning.

Dewey explains that in a world of constant flux with no room to make meaning it negates the live creature's capacity to achieve resolutions. He further explains that in a world where the reverse is true, with everything predetermined, there would be no fulfillment: "In a finished world, sleep and waking could not be distinguished" (p. 17). And yet, it is the finished world of the classroom that students often meet as curriculum is separated from self-understanding. With little to no attention given for students' curiosities, suggestions, and order seeking, students are rarely positioned to assimilate, internalize, and integrate their thinking. Instead, curricular experiences compartmentalize knowledge, separating pedagogy from content, and knowledge from interests. Finished meanings are determined in advance for all. Therefore, *alibis in being* are fostered.

Contrarily, the Floodwall Project invites personal investment, confronting and challenging self-understanding. It cultivates the contextual conditions and criteria to foster and nurture the agentic consequences of human curiosity, suggestion, and orderliness as productive for all that participate, "because [such] experience is the fulfillment of an organism in its struggles and achievements in a world of things, it is art in germ" (Dewey, 1934, p. 19). Curiosity, suggestion, and orderliness, intrinsic within aesthetic play, germinate within teaching/learning situations. Barone (1983) claims this is so, "even when dormant or struggling to germinate" (p. 26). Curricular conversations become meaning-full as connections develop through curiosities, inciting suggestions, and finding order, through creating, responding, and relating alongside other(s). Opportunities are then afforded for challenging personal assumptions, values, and beliefs. Identities are fostered that are in touch with self and contexts. Personal learning agency is gained through such connectedness. Dewey (1934) sees agency as central to human flourishing. To be fully human is to be alive, embracing thinking and feeling, seeing and acting. And, to access such agency, the role and place of curiosity, suggestion, and orderliness, as given human resources for inquiry of all kinds, seems counter-productive to ignore.

Curricular conditions and criteria must not "obstruct, deflect, and prevent vital interaction" (Dewey, 1934, p. 132) within learning contexts. The Floodwall Project powerfully reveals how:

> Through art, meanings of objects that are otherwise dumb, inchoate, restricted, and resisted are clarified and concentrated, and not by thought working laboriously upon them, nor by escape into a world of mere sense, but by creation of a new experience ... but whatever path the work of art pursues, it ... keeps alive the power to experience the common world in its fullness. It does so by reducing the raw materials of that experience to matter ordered through form.
>
> *Dewey, 1934, p. 133*

It is the deliberate play of individuals' curiosities, suggestions, and order seeking that holds the vitality, profundity, and continuity constituting the resources for matter to become form across learning of all kinds.

Postscript

The drawers from the Floodwall Project were exhibited in multiple locations, including traveling to New York City, and Berlin and Bremerhaven, Germany. These exhibits put people in touch with the narratives of experience from New Orleans. All 700 drawers returned to New Orleans and were erected into a pyre on the West Bank of the Mississippi River at Algiers Point. The location purposefully marked the failure of the levee-system in Hurricane Katrina. The pyre was intentionally constructed as a symbol of hope and forgiveness. On December 3, 2011, at 8:00 p.m., a cremation of the sculptural and conceptual pyre brought these narratives into a collective voice offering some closure, returned to the sea. As New Orleans currently rebuilds, the cremation was in part celebratory, but also a poignant reminder. The drawers folded into the moving waters the deeply shared understandings of loss that have been lived, and live on. Attention turns from personal loss toward the costs to communities. The Floodwall Project website (www.floodwall.org) tells multiple stories and prompts many more.

4

EMBRACING OF PLACE

FIGURE 4.1 *Broadening Space: Homage to Goldsworthy*, Stephanie Baer, 2011.

> The artist does his [*sic*] thinking in the very qualitative media he [*sic*] works in, and the terms lie so close to the object that he is producing that they merge directly into it.
>
> *Dewey, 1934, p. 16*

The notion of "embracing place" is compelling to me, opening up many possibilities for teaching, learning, and living. I was particularly struck by the wisdom of "embracing place" relayed by Cynthia Chambers (2006, 2008) as she described her personal journey to this realization and the implications for her curricular practices as a teacher and the common ground to be gained for the curriculum field. It is a wisdom that is only disclosed through embracing. But embracing insists on surrender to place. And surrendering to place demands trust in process. Curricular practices and policies for some time have ensured such wisdom is more likely to go unseen. Thus, as it entails curricular terrain that is apt to be foreign, the wisdom found within place goes undisclosed.

Site-specific artists and associated artworks deliberately embrace place. I turn to these works for insights into the wisdom to be found there. These artists share a reverence for what each place offers. Each place has a history with traditions, beliefs, and practices. Each place has unique features, phenomena, and inhabitants. And each place has particular elements characterizing the site/landscape and patterns such as time, uses, and weather that leave their marks. An energy or spirit exudes from every place that site-specific artists value, experience, and respond to caringly. The purposes and expressions take multiple forms, but revering and conversing with place is the necessary starting position for site-specific artists. Entering into a conversation with place entails inherence in the sensible. I am reminded of Yinger's (1988) attention to the etymology of conversation—*conversari*, meaning to dwell—suggesting "conversation involves entering into and living with a situation and its participants" (p. 1). It is this willingness to enter and dwell within the relationships already at play that embracing place assumes. It is within the apprehension of these relationships that site-specific artists find and create meanings. These site-specific artworks invite what Risser (1997) terms "poetic dwelling" (p. 199), instilling what Gadamer (1986) terms a "hold upon nearness" (p. 13). But what do these artworks bring us near to? This chapter first explores this question through the imagery of the site-specific artist Andy Goldsworthy, and the documentary (2004) of his sculptural forms in the making, *Rivers and Tides: Working with Time*. Accompanying this exploration, the educational philosophy of John Dewey (1934, 1938), with his concern for the primacy of experience to living and learning, is introduced throughout to form "crossings," with each text vivifying the other. Thus, both texts make more tangible Chambers' (2006, 2008) notion of embracing place as the generative ground integral to entering into conversation with place and bringing readers near to its wisdom for curricular practices. Second, this chapter addresses the question: What does embracing place entail for curricular enactment? The chapter concludes by considering the necessary educator sensibilities for navigating such curricular terrain.

Conversing within Place: Experiential In-Sites/Sights

Goldsworthy, a Scottish sculptor with a particular fascination with site-specific artworks, documents his artistic thinking/making experiences through the documentary film *Rivers and Tides: Working with Time* (2004). An impetus undergirding all of his art-making is voiced in his statement "I feel a need to understand the energy flowing through the landscape" (scene 1). No matter the place, this focused attention toward the particularities moving within the given landscape is where he begins all site-specific artworks. Dewey (1934) states that "Moments and places, despite physical limitations and narrow localization, are charged with accumulations of long-gathering energy" (p. 24). Both Goldsworthy and Dewey draw attention toward the relationships that resist, nurture, and sustain such experiences of embracing place. Goldsworthy examines, gathers, and converses with the materials of particular landscapes and creates sculptural forms, always cognizant of the flow that characterizes place. So, reeds and grasses from a shoreline form a giant web-like structure ready to collapse with the right burst of wind, tide change, or other inevitable interruption. Thus, Goldsworthy's forms are continually in process. He states:

> My touch looks into the heart of nature; most days I don't even get close. These things are all part of the transient process that I cannot understand unless my touch is also transient—only in this way can the cycle remain unbroken and the process complete.
>
> *www.rwc.uc.edu/artcomm/web/w2005_2006/maria_Goldsworthy/philosophy.*
> *html*

Goldsworthy (2004) is cognizant of being part of the existing movement of the landscape. It is this "transient" movement that informs how each artwork develops and transforms. The documentary, *Rivers and Tides*, brings viewers near to this movement of thinking, what Dewey (1934) terms the *undergoings* and *doings* within experience (p. 44). Goldsworthy takes an interest in the materials he finds. He works with their distinct qualities and relations to each other as his art forms emerge. The attributes of the materials, their interdependence on each other, their tensions and sustenance for each other, their strengths and vulnerabilities, are all revealed through engagement in process. As Dewey (1934) states, "The artist does his [*sic*] thinking in the very qualitative media he [*sic*] works in, and the terms lie so close to the object that he is producing that they merge directly into it" (p. 16).

The nearness to the *undergoings* (demanding an open, vulnerable, receptive stance) alongside the *doings* (entailing responding, organizing, discerning actions) of Goldsworthy's (2004) sculptures in progress that the imagery of the film provides, makes visible the patterns and structures unique to each experience. Dewey (1934) describes how the undergoings and doings are not simply alternating ways of operating, but rather it is the relationship that generates meaning. Dewey explains: "The action and its consequence must be joined in perception" (p. 44). The film depicts Goldsworthy attending to the materials he finds and incorporates. He relays how the materials "talk" to him and how, through study, he gets to know the materials more fully. The sculptural forms grow in proportion to his understandings of the materials. And these materials are "openings into the processes of life within and around it" (www.rwc.uc.edu/artcomm/web/w2005_2006/maria_Goldsworthy/philosophy.html). Thus, all understandings are situated within the given context.

Goldsworthy (2004) perceives his way into a landscape, sensitive and alert to materials, contexts, and the relationships that ensue. For example, in scene 2 the film depicts Goldsworthy before morning's dawn, standing amidst cliffs on a snow-covered edge, close to the sea. Goldsworthy is forming small cylinders of snow and joining them together to weave through a stark rock on the cliff's edge, jutting toward the sky. He comments that despite the cold he must be in close contact with the snow as he shapes and connects each cylinder. The snow cylinders turn to ice as he joins each to the other via melted snow and the workings of his hands. The spiraling ice form reaches around, through, and beyond the rock, coiling dramatically into the sky. As the sun rises and shines on both sides of the form, Goldsworthy enjoys the intensity of the illuminated form and expresses his delight in the unexpected contribution of the sun's encompassing presence and vivifying effect. But he is also cognizant that the solidity of the form is momentary and that as the sun continues to rise, some movement within the form will be evidenced, reshaping the form again as the cold night air returns.

Dewey (1934) describes perceiving experiences akin to Goldsworthy's to be like a "rhythm of intakings and outgivings." Working with time permeating place, the rhythm's succession is punctuated "by the existence of intervals, periods in which one phase is ceasing and the other is inchoate and preparing" (p. 56). The etymology of interval (returning to its Latin roots) refers to a metaphoric sense of "gap in time." Goldsworthy (2004) terms these gaps "cycles of turning" (scene 3). The film provides opportunities for the viewer to access how these "cycles" or "gaps in time" punctuate the relational movement of intakings and outgivings concomitantly working with time as past, present, and future fold into every moment. Their co-dependence is revealed in Goldsworthy's increasingly refined sensitivity to the particular qualities of the snow and ice, directing the shape the whole sculpture takes. Their co-dependence is observed in the receptivity Goldsworthy demonstrates as he surrenders to what the frozen landscape and the workings within it offer. Their co-dependence is evidenced as Goldsworthy works closely and caringly with one small part and then steps back to attend to the whole. It is this receptive yet actively giving nature that allows Goldsworthy to perceive with potential.

Goldsworthy's (2004) genuine excitement is visible as we see his sculptural form catching the sun as it rises. He anticipates the luminous character of the sculptural form throughout its development, but the sun's arrival just as he steps back from the form takes on a special intensity. Such co-dependencies across intakings and outgivings constitute the gaps in time or cycles of turning. They mark the "intervals" where meaning is generated (Dewey, 1934, p. 56). It is through revering and dwelling within, conversing with, and embracing place that Goldsworthy gains the vital intimacy of connection he seeks and the wisdom to be found there for his creations. It is a connection that he concretely achieves as he manipulates the materials of place, receiving what he terms "nourishment" (scene 1). The nourishment guides and sustains Goldsworthy's intakings and outgivings from within the experience itself. Dewey (1934) explains: "What is done and what is undergone are thus reciprocally, cumulatively, and continuously instrumental to each other" (p. 50). Such attentive trust within process encounters "gaps in time"; moments of fragile balance reached at the edge of collapse, "working with time," thus pressing forward into new understandings. Anticipating moments of balance between creation and nature is Goldsworthy's artistic task. Dewey (1934) emphasizes that "To achieve an exact balance of meanings that carry forward and pauses that accentuate and define is extremely difficult" (p. 173). Goldsworthy's embrace of place accepts the tensions, resistance, and discord as the expected difficulties alongside the wonders, pleasures, and satisfactions inherent within process. Rather than being disruptive, Goldsworthy understands process as being productive, uniquely forming experiential (moving) accounts of place.

Goldsworthy's (2004) documentary portrays the disequilibrium he feels when not in touch with place, disengaged from his surroundings. He describes such contact as devoid of conscious experience. Dewey (1934) offers further insight, stating: "The activity is too automatic to permit a sense of what it is about and where it is going" (p. 38). So, both Goldsworthy and Dewey disclose a rhythmic search for equilibrium, insisting on ongoing contact and communication. Both are adamant that it is this intimacy that is generative for learning of all kinds. Without such intimacy, learning becomes calcified. The generative terrain for learning must embrace place, insisting on the reciprocity of the spatial and temporal. Dewey calls it "space-time" (1934, p. 183). He explains: "Space thus becomes something more than a void in which to roam about." Space is temporally ordered through the "doings and undergoings" (p. 23). Images of Goldsworthy negotiating spaces recall how time "is the organized and organizing medium" (p. 23), instilling pattern, structure, and rhythm, thus catalytic to the movement it defines and creates. Dewey concludes that "Time as organization in change is growth, and growth signifies that a varied series of change enters upon intervals of pause and rest; of completions that become the initial points of new processes of development" (p. 23). The "initial points" of Goldsworthy's arts-making experiences are revealed in his capacity to see and act on the relations present and evolving. These relations become modes of interacting within the environment that enable him to attend to the movement of place from within the movement of the given living landscape itself. Dewey's distinction between seeing and recognizing emphasizes how important the capacity to see is in order to keep the movement alive. Dewey explains that recognition is perception arrested: "To see, to perceive, is more than to recognize" (p. 24). Recognition thwarts movement by labeling and categorizing, seizing identifications that distinguish and isolate. Over and over again, the film depicts Goldsworthy residing mindfully in space-time, embracing place, seeking agency through the relations themselves, forming and reforming generative ways to proceed.

Curricular Enactment: Theory–Practice "Relationality" Inhering Place

What the imagery of Goldsworthy's (2004) site-specific art-making in progress reveals so powerfully is its inquiry-guided nature and the necessary associated conditions, features, and capacities. The "gaps in time" presented through attention to process provide the relational conjunctures that generate the forms and directions each inquiry takes. It is this imagery that strengthens my understandings of Dewey's (1904, 1934, 1938) vision for education and prompts me to re-envision theory–practice relations within curricular enactment in classrooms.

I pursue working conjunctures that allow both theory and practice to better shape what teachers do in classrooms from within teaching/learning situations. Locating such theory–practice conjunctures entails building relationships across self, others, and subject matter. Learning connectedness is the necessary thread weaving these relationships and it is imperative that educators better understand its nature and implications. Dewey (1904) explains that the relational interplay within the pursuit of connectedness is a fundamental condition of mental growth. He states: "To be able to keep track of the mental play, to recognize the signs of its presence or absence, and to test apparent results by it, is the supreme mark and criteria of a teacher" (p. 14). Recent teacher education research (Cochran-Smith, 2003; Gallego, Hollingsworth, & Whitenack 2001; Mockler & Groundwater-Smith, 2009) reaffirms this importance. These studies point to the necessary conditions to support teachers' lived understandings of relational knowing and the connective potentials for learners and learning. A conclusion of Gallego et al. (2001) reiterates this need: "Without opportunities to develop the capacity for relational knowing, teachers and teacher educators will never be able to teach their students to develop such capacities" (p. 261). Opportunities and capacities are sighted through Goldworthy's (2004) art-making process. Their potential for learning connectedness lies within the "relationality" (Biesta, 2004, p. 13) found throughout the transient process that Goldsworthy lives and relays in his art-making experiences. The locus of education lives in-between Goldsworthy and his artworks, in-between teacher and learner. Biesta (2004) terms such in-betweeness "mind the gap" and argues that this gap is not something to be overcome, but indeed what makes education possible (p. 13). It is within such "gaps" or "cycles of turning" that Goldsworthy negotiates his artistic workings, evoking a boldness to proceed with care. Dewey (1934) insists that such care involves interrupting "our yielding to the object to ask where it is leading and how it is leading there" (p. 144). And, as Biesta points out, the direction entails both "risk" and "opportunity" (p. 24). It is this concern for the agentic possibilities of the relational interplay inhering place, the theory–practice considerations within teaching and learning (and life, for that matter), that forms the necessary tasks. The inherent risks and opportunities for the act of teaching are then understood as navigating the gap from within the gap itself.

Needed Educator Sensibilities and Capacities

Goldsworthy's (2004) artistic capacity to see and act within the generative terrain of place evidences the needed mindful practice Dewey (1904, 1934, 1938) envisions for educators. Davey (2006) notes four features of accomplished practice that return me to Goldsworthy's imagery, Dewey's philosophy, and the needed capacities that teacher education struggles to see and act upon. The four features characterize what Davey terms a "speculative sensibility" (p. 26) through (1) abilities to discern and reside within the givens of particular spaces; (2) knowing that no experience is definitive; (3) mindfully remaining in-between past and future, neither ceasing to listen to the past nor being closed to the future; and (4) approaching the future, continually cognizant of the potential it holds (p. 60). These features demand a "practiced receptivity" according to Davey (2006, p. 66), and it is such practice that the documentary of Goldsworthy's arts-making experiences bring forth. The features take life as we see Goldsworthy discerning and residing within places, receiving and acting as the situational/interactive workings of his art forms take shape, working with time. Akin to Davey, Dewey (1934) characterizes the necessary capacity as perception—an active searching alongside an intensely receptive activity.

Perception is the dynamic interplay that the act of creating precipitates. Perception and its complement expression are intertwined in Davey's (2006) notion of speculative sensibility as means and consequence, process and product simultaneously inform/form each other rather than alternating or operating distinctly. Perception, then, is a constant organizing and reorganizing encounter, guided by the anticipation of the sensible whole. The interplay discloses the practical wisdom, or what Aristotle (1925) termed "phronesis," living within the movement. Thus, phronesis is a form of knowledge that cannot be fully determined independent of situations and interactions. It asks one to reflect and discern fitting actions within particular circumstances and not how to ensure predetermined ends. To do so, perceiving necessarily embraces place. Thus, the terrain for sense-making demands intimate understandings of situations and interactions perceived within the unique movement of a given place, seeking wisdom undermining distinctions between being and knowing, matter and form, and means and ends. As such, place is a phenomenological notion. The mindful reciprocity assumed connects one to place. Place is the determining ground where meaning-making is generated.

Goldsworthy (2004) and Dewey (1934) call attention to perception's catalytic powers as a human capacity holding much significance for living and learning of all kinds. Its embedded features and conditions enable a vision of curricular enactment, with educators attending to the acts of teaching and learning from within these acts, embracing the reciprocities of making and relating alongside connecting and understanding place. Williamson McDiarmid and Clevenger-Bright (2008) point to evolving and expanding conceptions of teacher capacity. They conclude that at the crux of what teachers need to know, do, and care about, and how to acquire these things, is a "new appreciation for the degree to which teacher capacity and learning are social phenomena that occur across time and settings" (p. 150). Hansen (2005) outlines how the "ongoing attentiveness" that is demanded of such appreciation entails educator capacity to respond to place.

And so, I return to Chambers' (2006, 2008) notion of embracing place. Indeed, it seems it holds important sensibilities for teaching capacities, acknowledging and perceiving the social and contextual character of all learning that is engrossed in responsive, caring relationships. Through the insights gained through Goldsworthy (2004), Dewey (1934), and others, I deepen my understandings of embracing place. I envision relationships among students, teacher, and subject matter as the materials of place. The raw materials live in the experiences of students, teacher, and the subject matter itself. Attending to these raw materials and finding ways to build relationships connecting students, teacher, and subject matter is the work of curricular enactment. As these relationships between students and subject matter emerge and develop, the teacher's capacity to respond sensitively, fostering connections derived from an intimate understanding of students and situation, is required. Deliberation of these relationships is the indispensable play within perception. Curricular enactment comes into being as a manifesting, evoking, generative movement. It is not applied or imposed, but rather entails a relational knowing found within enactment that can never be fully anticipated.

Gaining access to the generative terrain of teaching/learning situations is essential for educators. A teacher's capacity to perceive fundamentally what is at stake in a particular situation—of what she is attempting to do when she teaches, the interactions between her and her students, what students are interested in and know, what counts and does not count within curricular enactment, and finally where she and her students stand and how they feel about being caught up in the unfolding action around them—is integral to being a teacher. But my work as a teacher educator indicates that opportunities to develop such perceptive capacities are increasingly denied and dismissed. Three decades (and more) of education policy focused on a flight from the experience of relational complexities toward representative certainty and singularity in ways of seeing, thinking, and doing in classrooms are resulting in dire consequences for learning. Teachers get little concrete practice discerning within the situated dimensions of teaching and learning. Consequently, a teacher's relation to curricular situations embraces the classical distinction of form/matter, subject/object, and means/ends through deliberately deciphering or ordering teaching/learning situations according to a preformulated script, rather than teaching/learning being about building relations across self, other, and subject matter, negotiating knowing within curricular enactment.

There is an urgent need to prepare teachers to see and concomitantly act with prudence, judgment, deliberation, and interaction, furthering students' learning within their practices. Relational complexities of place appear to be foreign to prospective and practicing teachers, and generally feared in teaching/learning. And yet, relational complexities are what generate the movement of thought as teachers and students constantly question what is seen and thought about subject matter as it unfolds. The vitality and play inherent within relational complexities reorients learning appropriately for learning's sake. Relational complexities hold the potential for bringing prudence, judgment, deliberation, and interaction forward as primary to seeing/acting within teaching/learning situations. Teachers and students need and deserve the nourishment found within generative in-situ teaching and learning. Teachers and their students are then continually conversing from within place and navigating place as participants "in an ongoing multi-referenced conversation" (Pinar, 2009, p. 11). As I take up the challenge of working alongside prospective and practicing teachers, I attempt to orient all involved toward these sensibilities and capacities found within and through embracing place.

5

IN NEED OF OTHER(S)

FIGURE 5.1 *Being in Total Control of Herself,* Yvonne Wells, 1990.

For the uniquely distinguishing feature of esthetic experience is exactly the fact that no such distinction of self and other exists in it, since it is esthetic in the degree in which organism and environment cooperate to institute an experience in which the two are so fully integrated that each disappears.

Dewey, 1934, p. 249

Yvonne Wells is a self-taught artist/quilt-maker from Tuscaloosa, Alabama, in the United States. Her story and picture quilts express narratives of personal and political experiences. She states: "What my head sees, my heart feels, my hand creates" (Exhibit Guide, *Quilted Messages*, International Quilt Study Center & Museum,[3] Lois Gottsch Gallery, 2011–2012). Wells insists that she wants others to attend to the experiences she knows to be alive in each of her quilts. Indeed, her quilts exude a spirit and energy that Wells characterizes as acts of expression that deserve attention on their own merits rather than being quickly categorized by style, tradition, or locale. Wells identifies herself as an artist, giving expression to her seeing, feeling, and making experiences as folk art, through the medium of quilts. She is wary of categorizations that too quickly gloss over the individual expression each quilt offers. As a self-taught African American quilt-maker and someone that distinguishes herself from other traditions, she seems keenly aware of the power and strength of her creating experiences as opportunities to negotiate self-understandings and give expression to these developing perspectives. A calling in Wells' voice, alongside the forms these expressions each take, permeates the exhibit of her quilts as displayed in the gallery as a whole. It is a calling that invites viewers to enter into conversation with her and her quilts. Wells describes her quilts as being "big, bold, primitive, and unique" (*Quilted Messages*, International Quilt Study Center & Museum, Lois Gottsch Gallery, 2011–2012). They are not traditional blocked or patchwork quilts and the unexpected big, bold, primitive, and unique designs are compelling. I find they draw me into their varied narratives of experiences, and the associated quilt titles suggest messages to me. The quilts evidence "the dialogic fabric of human life" (Bakhtin, 1984, p. 293). The narratives within the cloth invite further engagement with each one (see http://www.quiltstudy.org/exhibitions/online_exhibitions/yvonne_wells/messages0.html.).

"Clothed with Meaning"

Dewey (1934) carefully explicates the "act of expression" in the fourth chapter of his book *Art as Experience* (pp. 58–81). He evidences the developmental, unfolding process of self-formation and discovery that an education ought to entail and thereby express. To do so, Dewey emphasizes the primacy of being faithful to the intricacies and intensities of human experience itself. Wells' quilts speak to such intricacies and intensities within her life's experiences. And it is within the address of each of these works that Wells and others are transformed into realms not exclusively of their own making. In other words, self-understandings are interdependent with contributing historical, contextual, social, and personal factors in the makings of expressions of all kinds. Thus, although Wells clearly takes pride in her self-taught skills, her distinct artistry, and her passionate messages of spirituality, humor, politics, and everyday life, her quilts celebrate the human gift of personal expression that is "clothed with meaning" (Dewey, 1934, p. 75). It is evident that the quilts are not simply the workings of Wells' interiority, but rather, purposefully "clothe" her reflections, encounters, and stances as she negotiates the materiality of her quilt-making, disclosing the concrete realities of her life on a daily basis and within history. Such pragmatic commitment is Dewey's position, grounding the act of expression in the making experience and the meanings disclosed within. Akin to Wells, Dewey also steers away from categorizing and labeling, turning to the activity of the maker, the creator, the unique human being, having a particular relationship to all other persons, objects, and events in the world. It is this ongoing interplay "in active and receptive relation to the environment" that "holds together the various factors and phases of the self" (Dewey, 1934, p. 252). Thus, self-understandings always need other(s).

To further my self-understandings of the act of expression, I take an in-depth look at how Dewey (1934) explicates the act of expression through his words, alongside how Wells' quilts displayed in the exhibit *Quilted Messages* (2011–2012) explicate the act of expression through works of art. It is such reflexive interchange across both "texts" that Dewey terms a "double change" that "converts an activity into an act of expression" (1934, p. 60). It is the ground encountered in the double change that exposes the makings of expression the self gains. This ground, according to Dewey, begins with impulsion, acknowledging an interdependence of self with surroundings, learning through resistance and obstacles, and enacted at the junctures of old and new experiences (pp. 58–60).

Impulsion

Wells describes how, at times, the making of her quilts absorbs her attention wholly. The need to create and give expression to her sense-making consumes her with a felt urgency (artist talk, November 11, 2012). Dewey (1934) characterizes such creative flux as being initiated by an "impulsion" (p. 58). Personal needs and interests fuel the impulsions, as sustenance for these needs and interests is continually sought, folding into the making process. Wells' 1982–1983 quilt, *Raggedy Andy*, is the result of Wells' looking at the array of fabric scraps surrounding her, left-overs from quilting projects, and the felt necessity to create with them and find potential within these scraps (see www.quiltstudy.org/exhibitions/online_exhibitions/yvonne_wells/wells1.html). Their particular patterns, textures, and shapes voice her life's activities and remind her where she found each "fabulous piece" (*Quilted Messages*, International Quilt Study Center & Museum, Lois Gottsch Gallery, 2011–2012). She pieces and places the scraps of fabric so that they form a collective design and a useful product. Wells reflects:

> Each process has its own triumphs for me. Gathering "stuff" to make a quilt is very rewarding because there's no telling what I may find. If I see something out there in the street that I could use, I would jump out of

the car and go get it. Or, if something were lying around the house—my husband's clothes or children's clothes—I would use it. It would be placed in the quilt, and when the finished product was there, it was quite satisfying.

Morgan, 2011, p. 67

Dewey's discussion concerning the "live creature" (1934, p. 3), emotionally invested and guided by purpose and values, is very much alive in the workings of Wells' quilts.

Interdependency of Self with Surroundings

Wells' quilts convey the active relations and intersections she encounters in her life. Dewey (1934) talks of how human beings cannot gain knowledge of themselves without venturing into the world and exploring it. He claims that the self only achieves wholeness through seeking connections with surroundings. Thus, as Wells creates she is also creating herself, gaining new perspectives and ways to understand self in relation to the world. She emphasizes: "I didn't invent any of these events. It's just my interpretation of the events that happened during that time" (Morgan, 2011, p. 86). For example, Wells' 1990 quilt, *Being in Total Control of Herself* (www.quiltstudy.org/exhibitions/online_exhibitions/yvonne_wells/wells1.html), confronts how she felt when she first traveled to New York and saw the Statue of Liberty. She states:

When I got off the plane ... I saw that lady ... with her hands outstretched holding the keys, it looked like to everything. And, she was in control of everything. She had this other black person in her hand, squeezing it, with a piece of tape over her mouth so that person would be unable to speak. Under her feet stood the Indians, who were crying, "this is my country! This is my country!" and she steps on them as well, because she was in control.

Wells makes visible the exploitation she knows, and in doing so, challenges everyone to rethink how historical icons are storied and control interpretations that ignore or dismiss multiple stories of experience. She explains:

Stand back and look and see what has happened. I've had people say, because she was standing on the Indian, that was unfair. It evoked tears from a lot of people. That wasn't the intention, but you never know what people have on their hearts, and what their interest in the world is that causes them to have the kind of emotions that they have in response to art.

Morgan, 2011, p. 80

Dewey explains how these "attitudes of the self are infused with meaning" (1934, p. 59). It is meaning that gains depth and greater expression through deliberate attention to one's surroundings. Wells' personal/political experiences are embodied within the physicality and materiality of each quilt.

Meeting Resistance and Obstacles

Wells' quilts account for the things, ideas, places, people, and events encountered as she experiences these within her life's narrative. These accounts reveal the grappling en-route as she confronts resistance and obstacles that challenge her lived understandings. Dewey (1934) notes that it is critical that these challenges are understood as productive and not simply disturbances. He explains that such cognizance fosters consciousness of selves within the act itself of growing awareness of selves (p. 59). He further explains that if the route is always smoothed so that neither "feeling nor interest," "fear nor hope," "disappointment nor elation" is concretely experienced (p. 60), then learning is never known as a self-confronting and self-challenging venture. He cautions that opposition for opposition's sake is unproductive too. Receptivity, alongside a vigilant, questioning mode of being is needed. So, through purposefully confronting and pursuing the opportunities and vantages to be gained through confronting and challenging self, genuine action and reflection is fostered and a personal stance is cultivated. Wells' 1989 quilt, *Yesterday, Civil Rights in the South* (www.quiltstudy.org/exhibitions/online_exhibitions/yvonne_wells/wells1. html), juxtaposes depictions of Martin Luther King Junior, a lynching, the Ku Klux Klan, and a state capitol dome flying a Confederate flag. Wells discusses her quilt:

> Here [top left corner], this is the bombing of the 16th Street Church in Birmingham, Alabama. You only see three headstones, but the other one is behind the church. That's why it's not seen. Here [top left-center] are "Bull" Conner and the dogs they used to bite the marchers. And [in the top right-center are] the Klansmen in their [white-hooded] robes and their cross burnings. This [building in the top right corner] is the capital at the time, where the American flag was beneath the Confederate flag.
>
> And, this [one, the right-center] is Viola Liuzzo on her way to Selma. She was killed and she was one of the white martyrs that were working at the time. The Civil Rights Movement was not only black; a lot of white people lost their lives as well, which to me has not been elevated to the point I think it should be.
>
> *Morgan, 2011, p. 76*

These are Wells' accountings of living through these events and envisioning the impacts and consequences for herself, for others, and for the world. Juxtaposing key symbols and images that recall significant events and people, the politically charged quilt allows the viewer to see into Wells' negotiation of civil rights in the South and concomitantly call attention to personal understandings.

Lived at the Conjuncture of Old and New

So, as an impulsion initiates acts of expression, the elicited expression is not entirely foreseen. Interdependency, resistance, and ongoing reflection shape the messages that unfold. A recursive, temporal movement of past informing present with implications for the future is "recreated" again and again as "material is literally revived, given new life and soul through having to meet a new situation" (Dewey, 1934, p. 60). Wells' 1993 quilt, *Me Masked II* (www.quiltstudy.org/exhibitions/online_exhibitions/yvonne_wells/wells1.html), is the second in a series of three self-portraits that reveal a self in the making, continually aware of assimilating and changing through thoughtful action. Wells comments: "When I started off [quilting] I was making three of everything" (Morgan, 2011, p. 78). It is this lived conjuncture of old and new understandings that all of Wells' quilts evidence as they comment on events, tell stories of religious or historical happenings, or imagine new worlds, with all exuding the vitality with which she engages the world around her. An energetic and restless spirit is shared as the quilts express the ways she sees and hears others.

Curriculum as Reflexive Medium

Wells' quilts bring aspects of significant human experience to the attention of self and other(s). But her quilt-making does not denote self-expression understood as a solo, creative venture "spewing forth" (Dewey, 1934, p. 62). Rather, her quilt-making expresses other(s) and her relationships and entanglements with them. Her quilt-making gives expression to her world as she experiences it and interprets it. The reflexive "double change" mapped out above through impulsion, interdependence with surroundings, meeting resistance and obstacles, and living at the conjuncture of old and new provide "all the elements needed to define expression" (Dewey, 1934, p. 61). But what is often not understood, or is too easily overlooked, is how these elements become a medium for one's sense-making. Dewey (1934) explains that "the connection between a medium and the act of expression is intrinsic" (p. 64). Within the elements found through impulsion, interdependence with surroundings, meeting resistance and obstacles, and living at the conjuncture of old and new, Wells manipulates ideas, engages the materiality of her fabrics, and attends to the demands of continual judgments made within the making process. She is not concentrating on a pre-conceived end product, but rather on the act of creation itself. Expression forms through a constant interplay of reciprocal interaction and modification as Wells responds to newly discovered relations, determines ways of working, attends to modifications derived through these discoveries, and trusts her intuitions and the unfolding process itself.

There is necessarily a "lostness" and "foundness" of self within the act of expression, as Dewey (1934) states: "the live being recurrently loses and reestablishes equilibrium with his [*sic*] surroundings" (p. 17). Wells' quilt-making provides access to this movement of losing and finding self as she takes in, receives, and acts as situations call forth. In doing so, Dewey says, "We are carried out beyond ourselves to find ourselves" (p. 195). Gadamer (2000) claims it is such movement that fosters belongingness. Thus, in regards to her quilt-making Wells "comes to belong to it more fully by recognizing [herself] more profoundly in it" (Gadamer, 2000, p. 133). I find this too, as the quilts reach out to me, calling me beyond myself to find myself. The elements are living parts in relation to the vital movement of the whole. And these relational elements belong to the self and situation concerned in this movement. The centrality of the other(s) is, thus, constitutive of the self, and this belongingness is the connecting matter which becomes a medium where "no such distinction of self and other exists in it, since it is esthetic in the degree in which organism and environment cooperate to institute an experience in which the two are so fully integrated that each disappears" (Dewey, 1934, p. 249). All change in the process.

What Dewey (1934) terms the "remaking of the material of experience in the act of expression" is not just applicable to the artist. The "whole of the live creature" should enter into all learning (p. 81). A separate self is detached from the circumstances in which learning develops. A connected self is invested in the remaking of self—the experiential materials each brings to learning circumstances as each finds expression. Curriculum as a reflexive medium assumes all involved enter as creators, remaking through seeing, hearing, evaluating, connecting and selecting as "form ceases to be outside us as perceived and cognitively ordered material," becoming "an expression of a value-related activity that penetrates content and transforms it" (Bakhtin, 1919, p. 305). It is neglect of the reflexive relationship of self in need of other(s) that Dewey (1934) states results in deflecting, separating, and discouraging interactions with the world (p. 132). In Wells' works we see, hear, and feel the varied interactions and how, as Dewey states, these "things and events belonging to the world ... are transformed through the human context they enter, while the live creature is changed and developed through its intercourse with things previously external to it" (p. 246). Such reflexive relationships are far from mechanical. They concomitantly entail observing, doing, deliberating, and feeling. It is the opportunities availed through experiencing the reflexive movement of thinking that holds much curricular potential. Jackson (2001) explains that

> to be engrossed with what one is doing, to feel deeply about its meaningfulness, to undergo, even if only for a time, the near erasure of the

traditional distinction between inner and outer, subjective and objective, to feel as one with the object taking form under one's own agency...

suggests the significances for learners and learning of curriculum envisioned and concretely experienced as medium for sense making of all kinds (p. 174). The materials Wells works with change as she creates. Each quilt becomes a reflexive medium for meaning-making.

An Individual/Collective Movement of Thinking

Dewey (1902) asks educators to "abandon" understandings of subject matter as fixed, certain, and separate from students' experiences. Rather, he asks educators to conceive curriculum as a continuous reconstructing movement of thinking (p. 16). Akin to Wells' quilts, curriculum needs to call others into making and relating, perceiving and responding, and connecting and understanding. Curriculum as a meditating and reorganizing movement of thinking emerges from the personal negotiation of relations. All involved are positioned to question, attend fully, and remain open to possibilities. Curriculum then opens into a collective space for critical engagement of expressive understandings of self and others. There is room to wonder, to reconsider, and to gain insights from and through others that act as catalysts for the meaning-making movement. It is through attention to other(s)—other ideas, other forms of expression—that relations between self and other are continually addressed and personal connections and concrete understandings are meaningfully made and enlarged. Such a curricular movement is necessarily and concomitantly shaped individually and collectively.

Reciprocal, Connective, and Transformational Mediations

The individual and collective movement of thinking assumes content means little without engagement with curricular materials. Genuine curricular engagement manifests as a reciprocal mediation involving communicative interchanges across self and others. Genuine curricular engagement manifests as a connective mediation as purposeful learning is deliberately tied to previous understandings and orients toward future understandings. Genuine curricular engagement manifests as a transformational mediation as all involved change through the process. Through actively negotiating the mediations accessed through reciprocity, connectedness, and transformations, the curricular movement seeks coherence. Expressions of learning reveal the particular reciprocity, connectedness, and transformations at play, cohering process, product, and learner. It is the educator's role to prompt learning mediations that "sum up" and "carry forward" (Dewey, 1934, p. 169). This is Dewey's (1910) concern for coherence that relies on repetition (p. 83). The summing up addresses learners' tentative understandings through tracing the path to reaching these understandings, alongside questioning, validating, prompting, and challenging. Carrying forward addresses learners' tentative understandings through reaching out to new associations and interactions, coming to understand differently with more substance and depth. This summing up and carrying forward is both "novel as well as a reminder" (Dewey, 1934, p. 169).

Textured Curricular Terrain

Wells' quilts form the "coherent fabric" (Dewey, 1910, p. 83) that emerges through summing up and carrying forward. The *rich, related, recursive,* and *rigorous* discursive ground her quilts open into suggest the textured curricular terrain for all learning. Doll (2009) terms these the "four R's" that orient curriculum as a "moving idea" (Dewey, 1910, p. 213). Dewey (1934) envisions the moving idea as a "remaking" of experiences (p. 81). It is a remaking that calls all involved to reside within this curricular movement with sensitivity. Dewey (1934) claims such a capacity entails "Sensitivity to a medium as a medium" and he notes such sensitivity "is the very heart of all artistic creation and esthetic perception" (p. 199). It is this capacity to see and attend sensitively to the nuances and possibilities present in curricular situations and a willingness to play along with them as the givens deserving attention that characterizes the curricular movement of thinking, summing up, and carrying forward. Dewey (1934) warns, though, that extraneous materials must not be lugged in (p. 199). Attending "watchfully" and "thoughtfully" (Aoki, 1992, p. 25) to other(s) makes more tangible and visible the given significances of other(s).

Sensitivity to curriculum as a medium understands that curricular intentionality must create teacher and student dwelling time and space to find intentionality. After all, it is the other that asks all involved to see fundamentally the relational complexities at stake within specific curricular situations. Positioning students to dwell and invest in these relational complexities as orienting curricular situations is the necessary starting place toward building learning relationships. Teachers must reside amidst the complexities to locate opportunities to do so. Interpreting and acting on these opportunities may challenge preconceived notions and assumptions. Dwelling and investing within the given relational complexities demands curricular room to invite and foster receptivity and questioning, alongside curricular conditions allowing for vulnerability and boldness. But the more teachers and students reside within such a valued curricular space the more they will discern within the complexities at play. Therefore, trusting the relational complexities that learners bring to all learning situations is the ground that cultivates curricular richness. The interdependency across self and other(s) is concretely experienced and discerned as fodder for teaching/learning connections and curricular coherence. Richness is harvested through curricular dwelling, calling the significances of other(s) through participatory

thinking rather than lugging in extraneous materials separating curricular intentionality from the integrity located within the particulars of students, teacher,
content, and context.

Dewey (1934) also warns that the medium must authentically mediate. To
do so the medium must act as a "go-between" (p. 200). Through mediation a
contemplative space opens to negotiate freedom of thinking. Mediating the creation or invention of meaning through the positing of alternative possibilities,
freedom is experienced as a spirit of inquiry emerging of its own volition. Rote
responses, categorizations, routines, and hierarchal sequences succumb within
the liberating space to the relational dynamics and ensuing intersections as all
involved seek and give selves to the creation of meaning. It is the other(s) that
calls our very selves into question. The contemplative space to do so suggests
unforeseen possibilities. As these modes pull and reorient thinking, they question all that is involved. Dewey (1938) claims that the value of such curricular
experience "can be judged only on the ground of what it moves toward and
into" (p. 38). Ethical considerations are thus foregrounded. Curricular practices
that exclude, confine, and deny other(s) limit the relations that might act as
modes of interaction and deliberation. Dewey terms such practices "mis-
educative," so focused on external references that the contextual milieu is
entirely negated. Such negligence is irresponsible and privileges a predetermined
direction, dismissing many learners and "disavowing" learning (Taubman,
2012). So, the "educative" ground that contemplative space opens into is necessarily fragile, full of contingencies that paradoxically strengthen learners and
learning. Relations are then called upon as modes of interaction and mediation,
fostering speculation, projection, and invention of meanings, instilling what
Dewey (1938) terms "social control," with control coming from within the
curricular movement itself.

Finally, Dewey (1934) warns that sensitivity to a medium as a medium does
not divide the mind from experience. The curricular movement of thinking
must connect "ends in view" and means (Dewey, 1934). Thus, it positions all
involved to identify the overall curricular undertaking, but also closely identify
with the task itself. Dewey (1934) explains that this is how the artist works,
assuming the attitude of the perceiver while engaged in the making process. It
seems that only as ends and means are purposefully navigated and shape
responses can they form a continuum. May (1993) clarifies that ends and
means "are intertwined and interactive, in dialectical intention and reflexive
play, both perceptive and receptive, just as form and substance are inseparable
in art" (p. 216). Ends are thus not located in one place. Dewey (1934) con-
firms that "a conclusion is no separate and independent thing; it is the consummation of a movement" (p. 38). A greater sense of self emerges,
progressively articulated and unified through concrete interactions with
other(s). Meanings are reconstituted again and again through such recursive
opportunities to see and enlarge one's understandings. Gadamer's (2000)

association of play as a pattern or structure reconstituted by those who play along describes the immediacy of the relationality to be navigated alongside the potential to be gained for ongoing action (p. 110). Recursion calls upon previous understandings through a revisiting, reconsidering, and reconstituting curricular movement.

The rich, relational, and recursive curricular terrain encountered is embraced as fertile, generating an ongoing rigorous search for coherence and continuity. The generativity of the "moving idea" of curriculum teaches all involved to value learning as interdependent with others. Beginning with impulsion, acknowledging an interdependence of self with surroundings, learning through resistance and obstacles, and enacted at the junctures of old and new experiences (Dewey, 1910, pp. 58–60), teachers must perceive their way into the texture of learning situations and not away from them. Within this movement teachers and students can both seek and seize possibilities for curricular practices. It importantly calls teachers and students to live their lives in classrooms with greater sensitivity. Wells' quilt-making reveals such sensitivity:

> There are trials and errors because sometimes colors or pieces don't work together. If I'm telling a story here [in *Being in Total Control of Herself*], and I put a piece next to the lady and money and put both of them on the same side, that wouldn't say what I want to; color dictates, and what you're trying to say, dictates where a piece would go. But, I would lay it out on the floor ... that's where my energy comes from! All those shapes that are down there on the floor, all those colors, I get energy from that. I could look over there at a pile and say: "Ooh! That could be such and such a thing!" So I jump up and get that. I don't usually just sit there. When I'm working on a quilt, I think: "Mmm, I think I just need to go and get this. I think I need to put this right here." It's not complete when I pick it up off the floor and put it on the rack [quilting frame]. It's still telling the story as I quilt.
>
> *Morgan, 2011, Interview with Artist, p. 81*

Sensitivity to other(s) calls our very selves into question. Sensitivity to other(s) attends to the significances within situations. Sensitivity to other(s) incites a turn and return to self understandings. Otherness holds tremendous pedagogical agency for textured curricular conversations. Perhaps this is the liberating agency Wells' quilts clothe for all learning.

6

TEMPORAL SPATIAL AGENCY

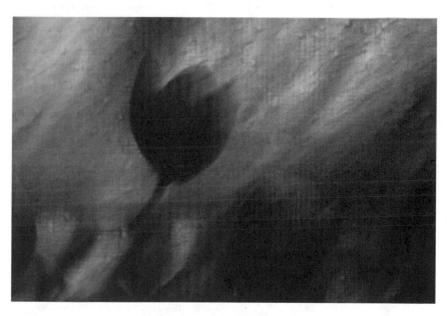

FIGURE 6.1 *Tulip: Agency of Time Series*, Leighton Pierce, 2008.

Space ... becomes something more than a void ... it becomes a comprehensive and enclosed scene within which are ordered the multiplicity of doings and undergoings in which man [*sic*] engages. Time ceases to be either the endless and uniform flow or the succession of instantaneous points ... it is an ordering of growth and maturations.

Dewey, 1934, p. 23

I enter the art installation *Agency of Time* (2008) at the Sheldon Museum of Art[4] in Lincoln, Nebraska with students from my curriculum theory class in the College of Education and Human Sciences at the University of Nebraska-Lincoln, USA[5] (see www.sheldonartmuseum.org/exhibitions/past_exhibitions. html). The artist, Leighton Pierce, is concerned with composing meaningful experiences in space and time. Such concern seems very fitting for curricular enactment in classrooms. This is the assumption I ask students to consider as they enter the installation.

Pierce (2008) explains that he works with interfaces in architectural space to "explore the collision and intermixing that occurs between multiple images and sound over time, across space, and within the associative mind of the viewer" (www.leightonpierce.com). The installation immediately positions all of us to enter into the experience already underway. Using images and sound, Pierce projects fast-moving video footage on three wide screens along one wall, and playing across and around the surface of a vertical column centered within the installation space. The experiential context incites inward personal associations while in the presence of engaging stimuli on the outside (Kennedy, 2008—interview with the artist). The students and I each recognize aspects of the stimuli and we respond in varied ways. Alongside the internal associations, the context invites physical movement within the installation space, but all move slowly and carefully, taking in aspects of the passing perspectives offered by lighting, sound, streaming images, and proximity. The low lighting, abstracted imagery, and somewhat familiar yet strange encounters makes for our tentative movements within the space. Each screen recursively reveals the same imagery, but reworked and reordered in continuous cycles. We catch glimpses of rolling fields, trees, flowers, a woman, a bench, stairs, and a tunnel-like passage. We hear rustling leaves and branches in the wind, water flowing, distant bells, and footsteps. The interplay of images within the installation space draws us into the experience. The soundscape similarly does so too. The familiar sounds intersect with the play of familiar imagery, instilling an overall tone and suggesting a narrative in the making, and yet all stimuli are moving too fast to allow for details and particulars that might reveal a fuller story. So, we find ourselves lingering within a fast-paced, motion-filled context, unavoidably interpreting as we are immersed within the experience created. Impressions emerge through the experiential whole of the installation. Individually and collectively, the students and I return to these impressions to consider the task of interpretation and its temporal and spatial play within experiences of all kinds, and in particular we seek implications for our curricular experiences as educators.

Temporality, as a movement of past, present, and future that figures into every moment, surfaces as a permeating impression of the installation, *Agency of Time*. All students are practicing educators and the installation positions them to confront how time as a past, present, and future movement is co-opted in their curricular practices. Time is something they acknowledge to be much more of a commodity or an entity than something experienced as temporal agency within their classroom settings. Time is a commodity that controls and accounts for pacing charts that outline scope and sequence, and short- and long-term curricular planning. Time is an entity that regulates and schedules time allotments for specific subject matter and related skills, and ensures coverage of material and time spent on tasks. Hunsberger (1992) refers to these time associations as "clock time" (p. 66). In fact, several students explain that "teacher time" clocks are encouraged in some settings to monitor length of time for specific activities and behaviors, sounding and flashing a "time's up" alarm. We discuss how, in clock time, the past is forever behind us and the future always before us, with the present given little regard (or even empty) because the finished, future product is the primary focus. *Agency of Time* provides an opportunity to consider time within the experience of the installation itself. Hunsberger posits time as a "flux of intentionalities" with future and past inseparably involved in the present. She explains how the divisions of past, present, and future "do not always serve us well" (p. 65). We reflect on how Pierce (2008) brought us into a space in which the future and past are experienced through the flux of intentionalities within the living present. Dewey (1934) explains that in doing so, "Time as empty does not exist; time as an entity does not exist. What exists are things acting and changing" within and through time (p. 210). Concrete access to things acting and changing within and through time is what Pierce's installation provides.

Spatiality, as the context entered through the world of the installation, is also a permeating impression. The installation is within a rectangular room, but the moving imagery, soundscape, flickering colors, lighting, and suggestive narrative creates what Pierce characterizes as "an acoustic coloring of the entire space" (Kennedy, 2008). Spatiality as an acoustic coloring entails transitioning from Hunsberger's (1992) "clock time to inner time and to a different sort of reality" (p. 66). Individuals' perceptions, emotions, and memories are called to the surface and infuse the space. The students and I are challenged to think of educative spaces beyond the rectangular room typically arranged and structured to minimize interactions, toward educative spaces cultivating "pedagogical tone" (Van Manen, 1991) and the realities of such a tonal space enabling and deepening interactive opportunities found within inner time. Dewey (1934) claims that "Works of art express space as opportunity for movement and action" (p. 209). Pierce's installation becomes such an opportunity for accessing the agentic possibilities of curricular experiences as spatial encounters and negotiations.

"Space-time"

Dewey (1934) explains that space and time are "properties" permeating every artistic expression (p. 206). He emphasizes their interdependence by terming it "space-time" (p. 206). It is the unity of space-time that the installation accesses. The concrete experience of space-time reciprocity offers unique structures for understanding in everyone that enters. We envision curriculum artfully unfolding through the spatial-temporal properties giving form to learning experiences. These spatial-temporal properties form the substance that Pierce reveals through *Agency in Time* as we reflect on our deepening and enveloping "felt relationship between doing and undergoing" (Dewey, 1934, p. 212) qualitatively inhering the installation as a whole. These inhering qualities of space and time reciprocally affect and modify one another. Dewey (1934) calls attention to four warnings that *Agency of Time* heeds:

1. "Space is inane save as occupied with active volumes" (p. 212). The installation is an active moving experience and all that enter the space become part of the ongoing temporal movement. We think about the lived implications for educative settings as sites of ongoing action and generativity. We pursue teacher and student capacities to attend to the fullness of understandings in any given situation. We seek the necessary conditions to foster and sustain curricular spaces occupied with manifesting the ensuing volume rather than diminishing it.

2. Pauses become "holes when they do not accentuate masses and define figures as individuals" (p. 212). The installation experience insists on involvement, inciting all to bring their own associations and interpretations to the foreground, negotiating varied rhythms of sense-making. The rhythms vary across individuals with "pauses, places of rest" that "punctuate and define the quality of movement" (p. 36). We consider how curricular space can accentuate and define pauses for integrating and internalizing a multiplicity of meanings. We envision making space for building upon these meanings with other(s), rather than the space to do so being sucked into holes or voids where one's involvement and interpretations are discouraged and hidden.

3. "Extension sprawls and finally benumbs if it does not interact with place so as to assume intelligible distribution" (p. 212). The installation experience comprises a parts-to-whole interchange that is continuous and blending. As part of this extending interchange, individual and collective participation values and seeks differences specific to place and participants as productive for purposeful encounters to emerge and develop. We reflect on the way in which many curricular practices that extend into multiple activities and sprawl out in multiple directions without time and space to locate learning connections can benumb all involved.

4. "Mass is nothing fixed. It contracts and expands, asserts itself and yields, according to its relations to other spatial and enduring things" (p. 212). The installation experience depends on the relations participants bring and mass within the experience itself. We are positioned to constantly question what

we are seeing and thinking about as the installation experience unfolds. It is the relations that generate the movement of thinking. We consider how the vitality inherent within these massing relationships could reorient curricular practices toward individual and collective growth.

Dewey (1934) states that heeding these four warnings—thus valuing space-time within experiences—entails a lived understanding of its productive reciprocity, where "Space ... becomes something more than a void ... it becomes a comprehensive and enclosed scene within which are ordered the multiplicity of doings and undergoings in which man [*sic*] engages" (p. 23). And "Time ceases to be either the endless and uniform flow or the succession of instantaneous points ... it is an ordering of growth and maturations" (p. 23).

Space and time are central to Dewey's (1934, 1938) primary notion of *experience*. The relational inseparability of space-time is at the nexus of Dewey's criteria of "situation" and "interaction" constituting experience. Situation is the "comprehensive scene" and interaction holds the "organizing medium" (1934, p. 23). Experience understood as such demands active structuring of what is encountered on a continual basis. A learning approach and direction is accessed from within the experience itself. Dewey (1938) terms such access a "moving force" (p. 38), and Pierce's (2008) installation heightens our attention toward the importance of situation and interaction enabling the spatial/temporal experiential agency of learning. The situation created by Pierce assumes interaction and immerses us in an experiential dwelling space emphasizing the present. Even though each present moment is fleeting, we are cognizant of the agency of space-time bringing each of us to the lived conjuncture of past–present–future, experiencing what is at stake within the present. The lived conjuncture positions us to attend to the particulars of context and relations. The lived conjuncture positions us to attend to the tensions and affinities. The lived conjuncture positions us to continually seek connections with surroundings. Our reflective curricular conversations then consider the costs of disregarding students' associations and interpretations during given learning moments. We gain greater cognizance of the present holding the complexities that come with being in relation within specific situations with other(s). We gain greater cognizance of how the present invites mindful, responsive attention to contexts, students, and subject matter as resources for curricular enactment.

The Agency and Potentialities of the Present

Collaboratively, the students and I discuss how space-time at play within the present is largely foreign within curricular practices and discourses. Dewey's (1934) warnings regarding space-time are not seen, never mind heeded. It is such blindness that we discuss as contributing to what Hargreaves and Shirley (2009) term "endemic," "adaptive," and "addictive" curricular translations.

Endemic translations result from the ways schools and classrooms are organized, concerned primarily with effective large-group management, controlling the movement of students from activity to activity, class to class, and grade to grade with little to no regard for the space-time at play within these settings (pp. 2508–2509). Adaptive translations manifest as large-scale education reform initiatives that position teachers and students to focus on end products with no space-time to negotiate meanings (pp. 2509–2511). Addictive translations are the result of the relentless quest for short-term gains with school systems evolving into addictive organizations (pp. 2523–2526). It is such endemic, adaptive, and addictive curricular translations that deny the present and incapacitate attempts to see the costs.

So the curricular conversation among the students and I delves into the nature of the present that demands teaching reside mindfully at the nexus of situation and interaction while seeking the agency of space-time. Dewey (1938) refers to such mindfulness as "an ever-present process" (p. 50). Agency is solicited as educators' "immediate and direct concern" orients toward "the situations in which interaction takes place" (Dewey, 1938, p. 45). Agency is further solicited as educators acknowledge and address "the powers and purposes of those taught" (Dewey, 1938, p. 45). Dewey's (1938) discussion of the notion of "preparation" and its spatial/temporal character clearly articulates why the present ought not be ignored. Dewey states:

> When preparation is made the controlling end, then the potentialities of the present are sacrificed to a suppositious future. When this happens, the actual preparation for the future is missed or distorted. The ideal of using the present simply to get ready for the future contradicts itself. It omits, and even shuts out, the very conditions by which a person can be prepared for his [sic] future.
>
> *p. 49*

It is not that the past and future are unimportant, but as Dewey claims, it "is not an either-or affair" (p. 50). It is a teacher's responsibility to see and attend to the ever-present process in which past, present, and future are constantly mediated.

Considering how the potentialities of the present in many classroom settings have been, and are being, sacrificed to a suppositious future, absorbs the students' and my attention. Endemic, adaptive, and addictive practices consume much of our work as teachers. Confronting these practices reveals curriculum enactment to entail predetermined approaches with pre-established paces for telling, covering, and imposing content. But Dewey's ever-present process proposes a challenge for all of us to embrace the present, bringing the past and future continually to bear. The installation experience forced us to do just this, locating ourselves continually in relation to the present. It is this very consideration, questioning self in relation to other(s) (Smith, 1996) as needing space to form and time to be challenged, that resonates more and more with us as we grapple with Dewey's concern regarding preparation for the future that misses, distorts, omits, and shuts out the potentialities of the present for the future.

Agency of Time intentionally mediates the past–present–future concomitantly. Such mediation manifests as attention to the present, entailing a movement that recalls the past alongside a generative movement that evokes the future. Davey (2006), drawing on Gadamer (2000), describes how such conjunctures are infused with centrifugal and centripetal moments (p. 116). The fast-moving stimuli of Pierce's (2008) installation involves us in letting go of previous self-understandings (the centrifugal) and gaining new perspectives that reconfigure self-understandings (the centripetal).

Interpretation becomes the ongoing task that the students and I find we are caught up within, experiencing Pierce's (2008) installation. It is a task larger than each of us and not entirely in our control. It entails interpretive play that Gallagher (1992) describes as "transcending"—projecting possibilities—and "appropriating"—retrieving specific possibilities as one's own (p. 53). The cyclical nature of this interpretive play is concretely experienced in the continuous and repetitious looping of imagery and sound in the time and space of the installation. Gallagher insists that such a cycle is the work of learning. The play is never complete; it always moves into new and enlarged understandings. He explains that this is the nature of the hermeneutic circle, "sometimes expanding, sometimes shrinking, in the dialectical interplay," keeping "open the possibilities that define our experience as educational experience" (p. 80). Davey (2006) claims that keeping open the possibilities is central to Gadamer's (2000) concern with speculative sensibilities within the task of interpretation. We have come to see speculative sensibilities as necessary within Dewey's (1938) ever-present process. Speculation risks what you have come to know, thus it risks what you value, what you assume, and what you believe. Speculation requires differences to be embraced as opportunities to form, inform, and reform interpretive understandings. Pierce's installation engages our speculative sensibilities as we risk associations and connections in unfamiliar ways. It asks us to embrace the contingencies, tensions, and difficulties of difference as inherent within all undertakings. Speculative sensibilities thrive on the sustenance found within the risks and differences encountered. It is such sustenance that we find to be educative. This is the sustenance that we now seek as educators to occasion the kind of present that "has a favourable effect upon the future" (Dewey, 1938, p. 50).

Educators must be attentive to the "preparedness" integral to redeeming the present's potential. To do so, growth is understood by Dewey (1938) to be interdependent with space-time. It is the interdependency that reveals the needed sustenance for growth. Dewey (1934) explains that growth's organization is dynamic, taking space-time, invested in growing: "Time as organization in change is growth, and growth signifies that a varied series of change enters upon intervals of pause and rest; of completions that become the initial points of new processes of development" (p. 23). The curricular spaces for "time as organization in change" are the primary responsibility of the educator to create, navigate within, and sustain growth, according to Dewey (1938, p. 40). And he warns: "any experience is mis-educative that has the effect of arresting or distorting the growth of further experience" (p. 25).

Pierce's (2008) installation experience brings us face-to-face with the abstractness, multiplicity, and uncertainties alive within the present, foregrounding how growth begins with what is already at play. Not to do so, according to Dewey (1938), arrests or distorts "the place of intelligence in the development and control of a living experience" (p. 88). The agency and belongingness to be acquired are arrested or distorted over and over again as external control dictates much curricular enactment with no regard for space-time at play within lived experience. Indeed, curricular discourses and practices encourage educators and their students to detach themselves from the space-time circumstances in which learning develops. Such detachment strips pleasure, satisfaction, risk, challenge, and discomfort, and thus agency and belongingness are suspended, lying dormant. The dormancy refers to the "possibility of growth" and the "power to grow" (Dewey, 1916, p. 42). It is such possibility and such power which Dewey values as "immaturity," identifying it as a primary condition of growth (p. 41). For Dewey, immaturity suggests positive and constructive development rather than comparative assessments denoting lack. It is just such a stance that Nussbaum (2010) confronts in her discussion of how growth has been similarly conceived world-wide as economic gain, pitting peoples and countries against each other in competitive ways, concerned primarily with ranking, hierarchy, financial profit, and total control (pp. 13–26). Her argument outlines the deliberate global turn away from the arts and humanities, fearing the fertile space-time terrain encountered there for learning. Pierce's installation gave us a hopeful experiential glimpse into the potentials of space-time. We speculate about the agency that such fertile terrain holds for enabling the necessary habits and ways of being that promote human growth and well-being in a future made and shared with other(s).

Our discussion presses forward. The students and I consider how disregarding the ever-present process within curricular enactment as holding real consequences for the world's future is, perhaps, alarmist. A few students express their complete bewilderment from the onset regarding this experience of curricular space-time considerations at play within Pierce's installation. The connections to a curriculum theory course are difficult for all to grasp. Some resist. But we all concur that the space-time at play within the installation immediately engaged each one of us in the present, interpreting and drawing on our speculative sensibilities. And we are all struck by how much potential and power we encounter and envision for curricular enactment. We are taken aback by the permeating surprise and found hope.

The narratives of students'/educators' curricular experiences that emerge following our engagement with Pierce's (2008) installation hold something in common. All articulate varying degrees of feeling caught amidst the extensive preoccupation with education agendas, consisting of imposed education policies prioritizing high stakes testing. We agree that these agendas have not worked.

These practicing educators struggle to articulate what they are losing sight of and the reasons why this is so, typically seeing the curricular tasks of reorienting their practices away from and/or beyond such efforts as an impossible undertaking. Our discussion opens into how these agendas reduce professional action to causes and effects only, seduced by quick educational fixes and translating into concrete means or strategies with measureable outcomes (Biesta, 2007). We compile important questions about what is educationally desirable, alongside what is being lost and/or disregarded.

The experiential glimpse Pierce's (2008) installation accesses concomitantly confronts a diminished sense of educational knowledge and envisions it's potential and power. It is educative settings that have become dormant. The potential for growth and the power to grow hold the agency of space-time in curricular enactment of all kinds. Many contemporary thinkers relay how such agency can be gained through reorienting teaching from the "cause" of learning to the "context" for learning (Biesta, 2007; Green & Reid, 2008). But our experience of the installation reveals to all of us just how foreign the contextual considerations of space-time have become in classrooms. Davey (2006) articulates how "a practiced receptiveness and courtesy toward what is strange, unexpected, and that which lies beyond our most immediate cultural horizon" is critical (p. 66). The practice ground for such receptivity and courtesy within curricular contexts is entrusted with the growth of self and other(s). As educators, attending to growth means "care must be devoted to the conditions which give each present experience a worthwhile meaning" (Dewey, 1938, p. 49). These curricular conditions are alive within the interpretive, speculative, meaning-making of space-time, at play within teaching as an ever-present process. We can only find them from within such curricular enactment. But it is clear we are desperately in need of concrete practice locating and negotiating these conditions and valuing their lived consequences within curricular enactment.

Practice Ground

Space-time for pre-service and in-service educators to practice the teaching agency to be gained through teaching as an ever-present process cannot be itemized as a series of steps, rules, or procedures. Space-time needs to be experienced as wholly participatory; a way of being in the world that does not separate or distinguish knowledge from interests but insists on connectedness. The necessary conditions, insights, and agency for curricular enactment can only be found within the particulars of such space-time experiences. Agency can only be gained through ongoing judgments within unfolding space-time experiences, cultivating confidence and belongingness in process, and a lived language of practice to articulate these understandings to others.

The students and I increasingly see the potential within teaching agency as an obligation to the future, to resist the tremendous pressures of the future as calcified into predestined, representative forms. We increasingly see curricular concerns for generality and commensurability, dictating, reifying, and totalizing what is present, blind to what is absent, different, possible, and yet to be achieved. We increasingly see the loss of space-time within our practices as concepts are applied, framing curricular enactment instead of bearings being located, negotiated, and valued within the unfolding space-time curricular experience itself. Representations sever self from situations and interactions of space-time. Being-in-the-world assumes a situated self, interacting within the immediacies of space-time. But Britzman (1991) raises a warning that being-in-the-world is limited if an awareness of potential and given meanings are not cultivated along with a capacity to extend experience through interpretation and risk (p. 34). Her book, *Practice Makes Practice*, explicates this theory. The students and I look for ways to practice curricular enactment as being in the world. We seek ways to see more and more in the present givens of each of our classrooms as forming the ground for each of our curricular enactments. These reorienting efforts form the agency and found purpose that makes and reconstitutes each of our practices.

Reorienting curricular enactment toward space-time experiences continually meets contingencies. Such conditional, indeterminate ground is central to being-in-the-world. Boisvert (1998) explains that knowledge "grows with the varying circumstances as we become more sensitive to the possibilities that can be realized in the varying circumstances in which we and whatever it is we are trying to understand are placed" (p. 25). This thinking is rooted in Dewey's (1938) notion of growth and suggests the potential Britzman (1991) and Boisvert (1998) envision as key to being-in-the-world, plunging into the possibilities inherent within the relationship of self and world. The installation, *Agency of Time*, provided just such a plunge. Our ongoing curricular conversations have explored and excavated our findings. But it is ever clear how much we can gain from concrete curricular practice navigating space-time, and how much we are losing by lack of concrete practice.

As a means to further curricular practice attentive to space-time, Palmer (1998) compiles some practical ways for educators to reorient curricular enactment toward space-time experiences. Six paradoxes identified by Palmer become working notions for students and I to play with, immersed within the concrete realities of our classrooms. The curricular space-time paradoxes of being both bound and open, hospitable and charged, inviting the individual voice and the group voice, honoring the "little" stories of individuals and the "big" stories of disciplines and traditions, supporting solitude and surrounding it with the resources of community, and welcoming silence and speech, offer curricular play through enactment (p. 74). It is through navigating in-between these paradoxes that the conditions, insights, and agency for curricular enactment are encountered.

But the specific conditions, insights, and agency are fitting to the particular curricular circumstances. It is just such play that the installation incited, and as educators we collectively agree that such play is the needed practice ground for continual curricular enactment. Our shared commitment is to invest in further play, projecting possibilities and retrieving possibilities, reorienting our curricular enactment within space-time. So the investment in the future we initially pondered as being alarmist has become much more real, urgent, and we are ever more mindful of the lived curricular consequences within the present.

7

INTERDEPENDENT WITH IMAGINATION, INSTILLING EMBODIED UNDERSTANDINGS

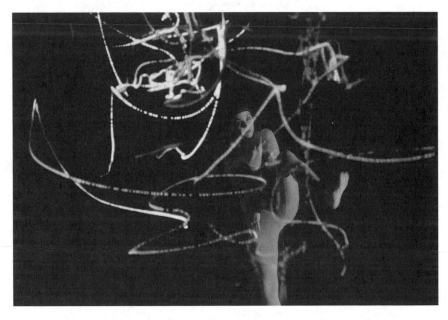

FIGURE 7.1 *Corpus Corvus*, Mixed Reality Performance, Heather Raikes, Julia Bruk (photo credit), 2011.

> The function of the creative imagination everywhere is to seize upon the permanent meaning of facts, and embody them in such congruous, sensuous forms as shall enkindle feeling, and awaken a like organ of penetration in whoever may come upon the embodiment.
>
> *Dewey, 1972, pp. 172–173*

Dewey's (1934) notion of the "live creature" (p. 3) as being in touch with context, moving and acting accordingly, comes alive in Heather Raikes' (2011) performance artwork, *Corpus Corvus* (see http://www.heatherraikes.com/). The body of the raven (*Corpus Corvus*) forms the relationalities where the immediacies of situation meet and interact. Absorbed concomitantly in thought, emotion, sense, and purpose, wholeness is continually negotiated and explored, binding the live creature to its environment. It is this ongoing pursuit for wholeness that is the work of imagination understood as a way of thinking with potential. Through Raikes' work, I gain greater cognizance of the body's role within all sense-making and how embodiment and imagination concomitantly unify and vivify alongside inciting speculation and the possible.

Dewey (1934) explains that imagination entails imaging forth interpretations living at the intersections of situation and interaction, derived from one's experiences moving into new experiences. He characterizes imagination as a "gateway," consciously adapting the new and the old (p. 267). Imagination is freed from strict understandings of static images and more fully experienced as a catalytic presence permeating the act of sense-making. This invigorating imaginative presence challenges persistent understandings of imagination as a special faculty of the mind, or a particular human gift. Instead, imagination permeates all conscious experience in varying degrees. But it is a slippery notion because of its complexity. Egan (1992) explains that imagination's complexity goes largely unseen even though it brings together "perception, memory, idea generation, emotion, metaphor, and no doubt other labeled features of our lives" (p. 3), the interactive workings of which are impossible to wholly articulate and unpack in words and distinctive qualities.

In retracing the history of imagination, Egan (1992) identifies myths' age-old capacities to envelop engagement in powerful ways that infuse memory and emotion (pp. 10–11). Contemporary physical-media artist Heather Raikes (2011) does just this, providing a way to access the fused makings of embodied imagination. Turning to the west coast Indigenous myth of the raven, she creates openings for the study of embodied imagination. Myths through the ages are sacredly tied to time and place. Multiple myths of the raven are known through their oral tellings within ceremonies, rituals, and social gatherings. Indigenous peoples tell many versions of this myth along the west coast of North America. The myth of the raven is central to Pacific Northwest Native American spiritual beliefs. Here, the raven is both a god and thief who steals the sun and creates the universe. The oral story-telling tradition of myths reveres time and place, and thus each telling renders versions that are creative, responsive, and relationally interdependent with time, place, and all participants. The myths' communicative tellings unfold through the developing reciprocities and ensuing connections, specific to each experiential encounter. Egan explains that such oral stories hold much power, extending beyond describing human qualities to embodying these very qualities. He states: "They [stories] hold up for us, and

(Dewey, 1934; Russell, 1998) and thus prompts associated movement and action. Through *Corpus Corvus* I concretely experience how multisensory engagement invites the translating room of *écart*, reciprocally fostering deliberation, intuition, anticipation, natality, and enlarged realizations. It is important to note that these suggestive modes are not understood as phases or linear stages, nor are all necessarily present within particular given circumstances. Rather, they are understood as latent sense-making mediums, often concomitantly experienced, and operatively and actively suggestive, embodying imagination.

Room for Deliberation

Operative and active suggestions encountered through multisensory engagement are deliberative in nature. Dewey (1922) characterizes deliberations as "dramatic rehearsals" imaginatively perceived as ways of moving and acting (p. 190). This experimental responsive activity is made visible and tangible through *Corpus Corvus*. Raikes (2011) experiments with technical processes to enable audience digital stereoscopic vision. She explains her compositional efforts toward the "superimposition and integration of a three-dimensional visual media layer in the physical playing space" to achieve "the illusion that the stereoscopic animation and the physical body are occupying the same depth space" (p. 7). The deliberations include the projected animations; the workings of the stereoscopic images in participants' eyes; the raven/dancer movement, positioning, and body; the uses of lighting; and the uses of sound; as the immersive experience forms and reforms. Elements of the raven's habits and impulses literally take "its turn in projecting itself upon the screen of imagination" (Dewey, 1922, p. 190). The liminal nature of the immersive context extends and enlarges the screen, becoming a sensory threshold to multiple experiments in movement and action. Dewey terms these "intra-organic channels," manifested as dramatic rehearsals (p. 191). *Corpus Corvus* positions all involved within the search for ways to move and act as the raven. Deliberation is thus catalytic and, as such, suggests multiple possibilities. Dewey explains:

> Nothing is more extraordinary than the delicacy, promptness and ingenuity with which deliberation is capable of making eliminations and recombinations in projecting the course of a possible activity. To every shade of imagined circumstance there is a vibrating response; and to every complex situation a sensitiveness as to its integrity, a feeling of whether it does justice to all facts, or overrides some to the advantage of others.
>
> *p. 194*

The sensory threshold of *Corpus Corvus* makes room for participants to concretely experience such a sensitive search "projecting the course" with the associated "order," "perspective," and "proportion" achieved through deliberation of competing habits and impulses (Dewey, 1922, pp. 194–195). It is this room to genuinely deliberate that makes room to embrace deliberation's flexibility, remaking old aims and habits and instilling love of new ends and acts (p. 198). Without embracing its flexibility, deliberations would be constricted and denied room to enlarge and deepen understandings.

Room for Intuition

Operative and active suggestions encountered through multisensory engagement are accepting of intuitions. Dewey (1934) understands intuition as the readjustment effected as old and new meet and sudden harmony occurs (p. 261). The moving sensory experience of *Corpus Corvus* entails such meetings of old and new. Participants' interpretations are foregrounded in "flash[es] of revelation" to be superseded by new flashes in a continuous movement situating self within the experience (Dewey, 1934, p. 261). The suddenness of intuitions often result from previous experiences in which the patterns, structures, and conditions within experiential encounters are familiar and yet newly encountered.

Raikes (2011) draws upon her personal experiences of studying with the dancer/choreographer Erick Hawkins (1909–1994) as she creates *Corpus Corvus*. The rootedness of Hawkins' thinking concerning the essence of movement as sensation embodied within dance manifests in Raikes' commitment to expanding embodiment beyond the body-subject to a virtuosic meta-bodily whole; an encompassing, organic, contextualized form (p. 10). Akin to Dewey's (1934) interpretation of form as inseparable from substance, "carry(ing) the experience of an event, object, scene, and situation to its own integral fulfillment" (p. 137), Raikes (2011) conveys how the underlying infrastructure of the performance artwork is conceived as an extension of the human nervous system (p. 11). The form is designed to both resonate and readjust as convergences are concretely experienced within the body-subject and the virtuosic body. *Corpus Corvus* draws upon participants' intuitions, vivifying the meta-body, merging consciousness and technology, and "the ancient history of human mythos through the prism of digital language" (Raikes, 2011, p. 13). Gadamer's (1986) claim of the vividness to be found within intuitions is apprehended through the immersive bodily experience of *Corpus Corvus*. Similarly, Dewey (1934) explains how this "marks the place where the formed dispositions and the immediate situation touch and interact" (p. 266), compelling all involved to "surrender" and "reflect" (p. 53). The vivid bodily memory marks the intuition. The "imprint" left (Bowman, 2004, p. 46) forms the substance of internalized understandings. The sensory threshold of *Corpus Corvus* makes room for intuition to manifest and make such internalized marks. Richmond and Snowber (2009) characterize the intimacy that is gained as the value of embodied understandings (p. viii).

Room for Anticipation

Operative and active suggestions encountered through multisensory engagement foster anticipation. Abrams (1996) conveys how "the senses throw themselves beyond what is immediately given, in order to make tentative contact
with the other sides of things that we do not sense directly, the hidden or invisible aspects of the sensible" (p. 58). Such throwing beyond is characterized as
anticipation, an ongoing parts-to-whole movement toward a close that Dewey
(1934) explains "does not wait in consciousness for the whole understanding to
be finished. It is anticipated throughout and is recurrently savored with special
intensity" (p. 55). Anticipation, then, is a capacity to envision and re-envision
and, as such, is a "connecting link" (Dewey, 1934, p. 50) offering guidance
from within the experience itself. This guidance is found amidst the search for
"continuity," "cumulation," "conservation," and ensuing "tensions" of the
anticipatory experiential terrain (Dewey, 1934, p. 138). Therefore, as Dewey
states, "What is done and what is undergone are thus reciprocally, cumulatively,
and continuously instrumental to each other" (p. 50). *Corpus Corvus* provides
the "experiential avenues" (Baldacchino, 2009, p. 102) to move within such
reciprocal, cumulative, and continuous moments, anticipating moments ahead.
   Raikes (2011) explains that:

> The sensate body of the Corpus Corvus loops from the wholly kinesthetic
> spine of the performer-as-animal through its extended digital peripheries.
> This pulsation is the lifeforce of the Corpus Corvus, and reaches toward
> an integrated continuum of sensate embodiment that extends from the
> animalic to the immaterial.
>
> *p. 1*

It is the "loops" Raikes refers to that unfold the potentialities lying within the
developing movement. Raikes conveys the pulsation of the lifeforce as accessing
the interchanges of such movement. Baldacchino (drawing on Greene, 1995;
Dewey, 1934, 1938) associates the anticipations involved in such movement as
the dynamics of growth (2009, p. 102). It seems anticipation is growth-
inducing, with experiences "both tak[ing] up something from those which have
gone before and modif[ying] in some way the quality of those which come
after" (Dewey, 1938, p. 35). The anticipatory ground for growth is temporal
and developmental in Dewey's (1938) vision, and *Corpus Corvus* induces such
Deweyan growth through looping interactions, connections, and the search for
ongoing continuity, with past informing present, and pushing forward into the
future.

Room for Natality

Operative and active suggestions encountered through multisensory engagement birth new ideas. Dewey (1934) claims that "There is always some measure of adventure in the meeting of mind and the universe, and this adventure is, in its measure, imagination" (p. 267). Thus, the venture of imagination happens when diverse materials of sensory engagement alongside the search for meaning "come together in a union that marks a new birth in the world" (p. 267). Arendt (1958) partners such natality with plurality, the fundamental nature of being human such that "nobody is ever the same as anyone else who ever lived, or will live" as "the condition of human action" (p. 7). This condition for human action acknowledges the complexity of relations present in any given situation. Sidorkin (2002) claims that it is this capacity to see the relational complexities that "result from plurality, from tension born of difference" (p. 98). Dewey (1934) similarly conceives tension's productive role within birthing or natality as an elemental energy alive within plurality (p. 60). *Corpus Corvus* enacts such energy. Raikes (2011) explains: "Its mixed reality enactment ensues from a physical body in symbiotic dialogue with an expanded, immersive stereoscopic reflection of itself dynamically composing and decomposing in time and space" (p. 8). She composes and decomposes a relational multi-dimensional field for all participants to enter and immerse within, meeting resistance, and seeking identification, toward "bodily grasping it" (Dewey, 1934, p. 268).

I come to grasp the raven as a hybrid animal, human, and god, embodying creation, change, and adaptability. Such grasping is the work of natality, understood by Dewey (1934) to be interdependent with "the old, the stored material" as "literally revived, given new life and soul through having to meet a new situation" (p. 60). Greene (1995) makes it clear how this bodily grasping stirs "wide-awakeness," making empathy possible through a renewed consciousness of possibility, within a community always in the making, seeking "illuminations" and "epiphanies" birthed through "releasing the imagination." Thus, plurality in *Corpus Corvus* is "concerned with extending and expanding embodied intelligence through sensation" (Raikes, 2011, p. 11). A body of experience is collectively grasped. The significances of this collective grasping are noted in Arendt's (1958) warning that those deprived of attending to the plurality of others and vice versa

> are all imprisoned in the subjectivity of their own singular experience, which does not cease to be singular if the same experience is multiplied innumerable times … seen only under one aspect and is permitted to present itself in only one perspective.
>
> *p. 58*

Room for Enlarging Realizations

Operative and active suggestions encountered through multisensory engagement instill enlarged realizations. Dewey (1934) explains:

> We live in a world in which there is an immense amount of organization, but it is an external organization, not one of the ordering of a growing experience, one that involves moreover, the whole of the live creature, toward a fulfilling conclusion.
>
> *p. 81*

Corpus Corvus positions all involved to reside within the experience as sense-makers seeking organization from within the immersive experience itself. Thus, it involves us accommodating and adapting as we concretely participate through ongoing contact and communication. Dewey articulates the pauses and places of rest that punctuate and characterize the moving experience as offering moments of consummation that move into new moments (p. 36). He reveals how "art celebrates with peculiar intensity the moments in which the past reinforces the present and in which the future is a quickening of what now is" (p. 18). This is the vitality awakened in *Corpus Corvus*, with tentative realizations reached within the pauses and places of rest, summing up and moving on through contact and communication, resulting in conclusions understood in Deweyan terms as the consummation of the movement, and not as separate and independent things (p. 38).

The genesis of *Corpus Corvus* gives poetic expression to this "moving force" (Dewey, 1938, p. 38). Raikes (2011) clarifies: "The emerging poetics is, arguably, a whole greater than the sum of its parts, and something that can only be fully expressed in the experience of the artwork" (p. 2). Realizations are enlarged and deepened as "moving variations" are experienced as "subtle shadings of a pervading and developing hue" (Dewey, 1934, p. 37). As Raikes states, "Corpus Corvus ... provides a comprehensive account of its process of becoming—with the intention of both articulating groundwork for its ensuing poetic system, and evoking a sensate understanding of its experiential intent" (p. 2). It is a process interdependent with other(s). As Dewey (1934) explains, all change in the process: "In an experience, things and events belonging to the world, physical and social, are transformed through the human context they enter, while the live creature is changed and developed through its intercourse with things previously external to it" (p. 246).

Imagination evidences, through the search for unity across internal and external interactions, "inner and outer vision." Dewey concludes: "As imagination takes form, the work of art is born" (p. 268). It is the possibilities embedded within the art form of *Corpus Corvus* that illuminate the nature of embodied imagination.

Lack of Curricular Room Denies Curricular Life

A teaching/learning body that embodies the curricular movement of thinking within educative settings perceives the relational giveness latent within situations. Through multisensory engagement, room for deliberation, intuition, anticipation, natality, and enlarged realizations, opens, allowing for the formation of suggestions. These are the suggestions in touch with the particulars and processes of actual teaching/learning curricular experiences. Merleau-Ponty (1968) insists on the primacy of perception as a capacity to see and act on the ensuing interactions and relations as a communicative medium. But most educative settings and teacher education programs typically emphasize conceptual knowledge and dangerously reduce curricular practices to methods and strategies alone, with little or no concern for perceptual capacities. It is this lack of room to live within and practice embodying curriculum as a perceiving movement of thinking within educative settings that has contributed to these capacities becoming increasingly foreign to teachers, students, and the greater community.

Corpus Corvus brings me near to the fused makings of embodied imagination's pivotal role within curricular practices. The raven enfleshes meaning-making as multisensory communications, relations, and interactions. Dewey (1934) comments: "Without external embodiment an experience remains incomplete" (p. 51). It is the need for concrete connection with the world that the raven reminds me to value, seek, and experience as qualitative unity, the flesh, embraced within embodied imagination. Separations and categorizations distinguish practice from insight, imagination from doing, purpose from work, and emotion from thought and doing, so much so that Dewey (1934) warns:

> We see without feeling; we hear but only a second-hand report, second hand because not reinforced by vision. We touch, but the contact remains tangential because it does not fuse with qualities of senses that go below the surface. We use the sense to arouse passion but not to fulfill the interest of insight, not because the interest is not potentially present in the exercise of sense but because we yield to conditions of living that force sense to remain an excitation on the surface. Prestige goes to those who use their minds without participation of the body and who act vicariously though control of the bodies and labor of others.
>
> *p. 21*

Alexander (1998) describes how such disembodied ways of being alienate the senses. He warns that disembodied ways of being have become the norm, so much so that we accept these maimed versions as typical, with embodied ways of being understood as abnormal (p. 12).

Alexander's (1998) "abnormal" reality permeates many contemporary interpretations of curriculum, and the consequences are vastly underestimated

(Macintyre Latta, 2004, 2005; O'Loughlin, 2006; Taubman, 2009). "Disavowed knowledge" is how Taubman (2012) characterizes the curricular consequences accepted as normal. Drawing on Freud's (1940) use of the term, Taubman outlines how disavowed knowledge is connected to psychoanalysis and builds a case for its relevance to education. While this chapter is not concerned with psychoanalysis, I borrow the term of disavowed knowledge, finding its presence but denied visibility to resonate deeply with lived consequences of disembodied curriculum. O'Loughlin's (2006) communicative, relational, and interactive aspects of embodiment are undermined, thwarting access. I see these lived curricular consequences manifesting through disavowing communication's expressive powers, self-understanding's relational possibilities, and pedagogical eros' interactive directions.

Disavowing Communication's Expressive Powers

Through alienating the senses, curricular room for deliberation, intuition, anticipation, natality, and enlarging realizations is lost, disavowing communication's expressive powers. Disembodied curriculum orients communication toward top-down mandates and prescriptions to be carried out, repressing and controlling participation rather than expressing it and locating the suggestive powers within the participatory body. Dewey (1934) points to communication's expressive powers, stating:

> Communication is the process of creating participation, of making common what has been isolated and singular; and part of the miracle it achieves is that, in being communicated, the conveyance of meaning gives body and definiteness to the experience of the one who utters as well as to that of those who listen.
>
> *p. 244*

Repressing communication thwarts such conveyance. Personal, social, historical, cultural, and political complexities figure into all curricular moments in spite of repressive or expressive curricular conditions. But embodied curricular conditions and practices look to these complexities to convey personal investment, revise understandings, and seek transformation, relying on the individual and collective actions to empower all involved. These are the "meanings" and "goods" Dewey refers to as "truly human" effects of communication (p. 244). Teachers and students constantly question what is seen and thought about as subject matter unfolds. Teachers and students come to see and concomitantly act with prudence and judgment within such participatory communication. The vitality inherent within communication's meanings and goods then reorients learning appropriately for learning's sake. Such communication avows conditional, indeterminate expression as central to being in the world.

Disavowing Self-understandings

Through alienating the senses, curricular room for deliberation, intuition, anticipation, natality, and enlarging realizations is lost, disavowing self-understandings. The suggestive agencies within these modes of being are thus rarely experienced as teachers and students "struggle mercilessly to fit themselves into codes and agendas that maim and scar the soul" (Smith, 1996, p. 11). Teachers and students go through the motions dictated by predetermined codes and scripted agendas that distance themselves from learning as integral to whom they are and might become. The disembodied knowledge they are positioned to see is separated from living referents. At an extreme, Sidorkin (2002) explains that learning becomes mutated, "learning how not to be" (p. 49). Embodied teaching and learning orients differently, insisting on self-understanding's agentic capacities for building relationships among self, other(s), and subject matter, continually in the making. It is an understanding of self that is social, always in relation to others, and the opportunity to explore the ensuing agency holds significances for all participants. Subject matter increasingly matters as the ground between what we learn and who we are intertwines. It is this ground that is marked by interest, care, and pride, alongside grappling with a lostness and foundness of self that avows self-understanding's participatory curricular consequences. Dewey's (1934) metaphor of the "live creature" speaks to how "the live being recurrently loses and reestablishes equilibrium with his [sic] surroundings" (p. 17). It is such interplay of a lost and found self that instills organic relations connecting education and self-understanding.

Disavowing Pedagogical Eros

Through alienating the senses, curricular room for deliberation, intuition, anticipation, natality, and enlarging realizations is lost, disavowing pedagogical eros. Van Manen (1991) articulates how pedagogical eros orients toward students' well-being and "transforms the teacher into a real educator" (p. 66). Such eros values the given relational complexities unique to learners and learning, with curricular enactment suggested through the relations encountered and interactively pursued. Pedagogical eros is life-giving and -receiving. But such reciprocal curricular enactment within situations and relations is limited if curriculum is fabricated rather than attending to the curricular movement from within the movement itself. Arendt (1958) explains how fabrication is distinguished from genuine action. Fabrication can occur in isolation, manipulating materials toward a preconceived end. But action is never possible in isolation, needing the presence of other(s) and constant contact with the world (p. 188). Pedagogical eros requires Arendt's notion of action. Aoki (1992) discusses the needed action as "tactful," following the pedagogic good in a caring situation. He conveys the "watchfulness" necessary to be mindful of the movement of thinking within curricular situations, relations, and actions attending to past, present, and future. Accompanying watchfulness is Aoki's notion of "thoughtfulness, as embodied doing and being," deliberately seeking students' well-being (pp. 26). Van Manen's (1991) pedagogical eros avows "love and care," "hope and trust," and "responsibility" in learners, learning, teachers, and teaching (p. 65). But these conditions are difficult to instill and sustain if curricular situations, relations, and actions are fabricated. The consequences of fabricated curriculum entail regulated learning wholly divorced from time, space, context, and participants. It orients toward performing and conforming to unencumbered exchange and consumption that disguises and even obliterates the visibility of relational learning complexities of all kinds. Contrarily, pedagogical eros is a capacity to enable and deepen learning connections among self, other(s), and subject matter, immersed within the living "relational field" (Sidorkin, 2002), deliberately interacting in search of fitting action. Differences then become more visible and avow enlarged understandings, multiple perspectives, and fluid, purposeful learning experiences that foster divergent learning processes and products.

Embodied Imagination as Means of Comprehension

Dewey (1934) is clear that our different senses must unite to tell a common, enlarged story (p. 21). This is what Raike's *Corpus Corvus* reveals so powerfully. Mind is denoted as "a whole system of meanings as they are embodied in the makings of organic life" (Dewey, 1958, p. 303), bringing thinking, feeling, seeing, and acting into relationship and interaction—the body is encountered as the ground of all communication. *Corpus Corvus* recalls the sensible ground occupied with bringing meanings into being. Bowman (2004) explains: "Knowing in any humanly meaningful sense is emergent from and grounded in bodily experience and continuous with the cultural production of meaning" (p. 48). Within the movement, attention is drawn to process—how one is creating meaning and being created. Educators are aware that there is much in the day-to-day curricular practices that robs teaching and learning of such bodily engagement (e.g., Anttila, 2007; Blumenfeld-Jones, 1995; Bresler, 2004; Hanna, 2008; Johnson, 2007; O'Loughlin, 2006; Snowber, 2007).

It is the rootedness of sense-making in the biophysical rhythms of the lived body that *Corpus Corvus* manifests. As participants become actively invested in sense-making, a collective sense of presence permeates the contextual whole. Baldacchino (2009) explains: "This is where the imagination is not just a matter of individual cognition but an activity of the mind that empowers us to engage with its larger context—that of the imaginary" (p. 128). Johnson (2007) articulates imagination's tie to the body, "connected to pre-existing patterns, qualities, and feelings" (p. 13). The imaginary room for deliberation, intuition, anticipation, and natality opens intersections for such patterns, qualities, and feelings, compelling participants' "surrender" and "reflection" (Dewey, 1934,

p. 53). Such surrender and reflection forms the embodied impacts, the sensible ground of expressive communications, self-understandings, and eros occupied with forming connections. But such bodily engagement is submerged in educational thinking and practices. O'Loughlin (2006) explains:

> Specific dispositions may appear to have been acquired mentally, that is at the level of thought. But, this downplays the reality that such conceptual schema, beliefs, attitudes are not merely "held in the mind" but are imprinted into the musculature, bones, organs, and nerves of the individual, the dispositions or capacities eventually becoming a function not only of the consciousness which has the specific ideas, but of the embodied individual whose corporeal identity now incorporates those dispositions and capacities. What this illustrates effectively is that building up the stock of ideas an individual has does not really tell us what she knows unless it taps into the manner in which that individual has learned to perceive, feel and behave in specific ways corporeally. It is the corporeality of dispositions-formation that is essential and it is precisely this understanding which is often ignored, but which must be activated.
>
> *p. 71*

Raikes' *Corpus Corvus* activates embodied imagination, conveying how the body can no longer be overlooked as the ground for comprehension. Merleau-Ponty (1964) explains that the body organizes and gives structure to the phenomenal field simultaneously as the world recedes beyond and transcends our body's immediate grasp of it. Comprehension is this reciprocal body–world relationship, with a creating, adapting, changing body-subject involved in "an immediate and communal relationship with the meanings of the world" (O'Loughlin, 1995, p. 340). The body is entrusted with negotiating this sense-making ground, perceiving its latency, and moving accordingly. Dualisms dominating the history of Western philosophy such as mind/body, theory/practice, internal/external, learner/world, and process/product are thus circumvented, reorienting to the "flesh" of learning. Inhering in the sensible "comes upon" embodied imagination and "awakens" the "penetrating" understandings to be made and re-made there.

8

ATTUNEMENT TO PROCESS

FIGURE 8.1 *Steel Contour*, Pastel Drawing, Patricia Cain, 2011.

Allowing aesthetic experience to tell its own tale.

Dewey, 1934, p. 275

On a recent trip to Glasgow, Scotland, I immersed myself in the makings of place. Glasgow is a place where my ancestors lived and which I hold layered impressions of through recollections of family stories and associated images. These impressions of place are re-made as I piece together some of Glasgow's history in relation to contemporary times. The spring of 2011 in Glasgow is marked by the opening of the Riverside Museum, providing a home for Glasgow's transport collection and offering opportunities for visitors to experience Glasgow's ties to its proud maritime history. Located on the banks of the River Clyde on a site where Glasgow's other river—the Kelvin—intersects, its story seems fittingly located. The museum's architectural design playfully entwines the stories of Glasgow's ship-building history with contemporary artistic, industrial, and architectural materials and processes. The building catches the sunlight with its polished zinc form that follows the line of the Clyde, wandering along its bank. Visitors are invited to wander into and through the museum as they explore Glasgow's history and reinvention.

Piecing aspects of place together, contributing to the makings of Glasgow, I happen upon an art exhibit, *Drawings (on) Riverside* by Patricia Cain (2011) at the Kelvingrove Art Museum. Cain's drawings document immersion in the making process of the Riverside Museum and extend to the changing characterizations of place over time and people's complicity, calling attention to the lived consequences of moments in time. I bring my newly gained perceptions of the Riverside Museum to bear. The exhibit creates an immersive experience as the creative and collaborative making experience of the museum are traced through Cain's detailed drawings over four years, observing and studying the structural and formative aspects of the building's design by architect Zaha Hadid (www.patriciacain.com/index.html). The drawings are part of a larger collaborative undertaking with four additional artists in which the exhibit takes shape as an installation with the collaborators working on-site, attending to the creation of an experiential whole. Cain explains that the exhibit as a collaborative endeavor is "entirely a product of the initial observation work and the consequent idea that process should be examined through process" (personal communication, December 2, 2011). She articulates how the collaborations were led by the knowledge that had been accrued through the drawing process, revealing how the collaborators became "a part of the project once the exhibition space was defined and there was an opportunity to exploit the idea of the collaborative processes used on site at the Riverside in a large exhibition space" (personal communication, December 2, 2011). The collaborative pieces for the exhibit at the Kevingrove Art Museum were then physically jointly made.

Cain (2011) relays her role as akin to a project manager, building collaborations with others as the exhibit takes shape. Ann Nisbet is an architect who brings and works with the shared concern for process as both Cain and Nisbet construct a wooden sculpture, plated in zinc, akin to the processes for the construction of the Riverside Museum, as well as those often used in ship-building.

Phil Lavery is a digital artist who experiments with technologies old and new as Cain and Lavery converse and respond to the evolving project. Alec Galloway is a glass artist who is fascinated by the possibilities of materials, and Cain and Galloway explore these possibilities as the workings within process. Rosalind Lawless is a printmaker who creates a body of work with Cain that conversationally engages the collaborative attention to making within the studies of architectural structures and spaces in search of relationships to the art form of printmaking. Cain describes the creative tension across all collaborators as integral to making of all kinds, and as alive in the Riverside Museum, recording the Clyde area changes navigated over time (www.patriciacain.com/index.html).

A parts-to-whole relational experience is tangible as I gain access to the interactions, complexities, and tensions at play within the lived accounting of the construction of the Riverside Museum. Cain (2011) describes how she is compelled by this collaborative and creative effort as mirroring "the working on-site collaborations that occurred" (www.patriciacain.com/index.html). Collaborative and creative energies are alive in the experiential whole of the exhibit and I find myself absorbed in the workings of these notions and wonder about their roles within learning of all kinds. As I delve further into the makings of Cain's experiential accounting of the Riverside Museum, I turn to her book, *Drawing: The Enactive Evolution of the Practitioner* (2010), for deeper understandings of the attunement of process that she seeks and reveals through studies of making.

It is Cain's (2010) study of making that recalls for me Dewey's (1916) study of the nature of method (pp. 164–179). Both Cain and Dewey turn to the primacy of experience from within experience itself to characterize method as always in the making. Cain explains: "My particular approach ... has been to examine how drawing as a phenomenal event can actualize and visually make evident the emergent aspects of its own activity" (p. 269). Dewey (1910) similarly explains that "experience as the perception of the connection between something tried and something undergone in consequence is process" (p. 166). Their shared concern for the nature and role of practitioner knowledge in relation to method as experience-based reorients practitioner "know-how" of all kinds in significant ways. Dewey (1934) was keenly aware of this, insisting that to understand experience one must concretely turn to aesthetic experience (p. 274). This is Cain's task, exploring aesthetic experience concretely as a practicing artist, "allowing aesthetic experience to tell its own tale" (Dewey, 1934, p. 275).

Cain's Telling Tale

Attending to the creating process from within the creating process of drawing is Cain's (2011) commitment. The mindfulness she exercises and seeks assumes entering into a discourse. The drawings bring me close to her conversations on

Riverside. Cain's drawings caringly record her observations of the construction of the Riverside Museum. Many close studies of scaffolding with exposed beams and rafters reconstruct the making experience. It is through her attention to detail, documenting particularities such as a steel contour, brace, and dovetail joint, that I begin to hear the interplay of context and materials with the stories of all involved throughout the formation of the construction project. It is this conversation made visible through drawing that provides access to Cain's own understandings of the experience. I am aware of her discoveries found through drawing itself as they become my discoveries, reflexively linking to sense-making for both of us, and extended to all who attend to the conversation at play. It is a conversation that embodies the very unique character of knowledge residing in self-experience. The thinking movement the drawings depict tell the tale, reconstructing Cain's experiences with past informing present and holding implications for the future. Cain's drawings give expression to this personal and temporal movement, inviting all viewers to enter the exhibit and recreate their own experience, partaking in the larger conversation.

The primacy of dwelling within context permeates the exhibit. It is not simply interactive. Cain's (2011) search for meaning literally draws attention to many relations and interdependencies that prompt further unanticipated con-nections. It is only through dwelling that these connections come to be seen and enlarge understandings. Cain (2010) describes this in her book as "the experience of making rather than prescribing the content of what can be known" (p. 267). Cognizance of this emergent nature insists on openness to the reciprocity, suggesting an organization in the making, derived through concrete inquiry and engagement. It is the dwelling space experienced through the act of drawing that unites means and end for Cain. She explains: "What is meaningful is formed in the interrelations between what one does and one's understandings of this. From this we make connections not previously recognized before, moving further to make sense of other unconnected situations" (2010, p. 270).

Similarly, it is the dwelling space of the exhibit that positions viewers to inhabit, making room for means and ends as viewers navigate their own inter-pretations, with the exhibit space generating an increasingly multiplex experi-ence. There is little doubt that through reliance on process all change in the process as attention is oriented toward "meaningful evolution of ourselves rather than focusing on the outcome" (Cain, 2010, p. 271).

Multiple ways of knowing and the dialectical relationships involved through chronicling the making of the Riverside Museum permeate the installation as a whole. Cain's (2011) drawings depict the intricate workings of the building under construction. The installation space juxtaposes these studies of making with film footage from the Scottish Screen Archive, depicting scenes from the 1941 bombing of the River Clyde. The concentration of ship-building in the area supplying huge numbers of ships during World Wars I and II made the Clydebank an enemy target. The importance of the river to Glasgow's history is glimpsed as the roles of engineering feats making the river more navigable impacted the growth of industry and commerce along its banks. Narratives of making and unmaking fold into each other. This constructing, deconstructing, integrating, and disintegrating account is complicated as contributing artists converse with Cain's drawings. Ideas and processes are engendered through a process of working together, in which Cain and each collaborator jointly embark on the making process.

Nisbet's use of building processes familiar to ship-building in her sculptural form recalls techniques and materials of Glasgow's maritime ship-building industry, still in use today. I learn that the Cunard liners, the Queen Mary, Queen Elizabeth, QE2, and the Royal Yacht Britannia were all built here. The sculptural forms co-created by Nisbet and Cain for the exhibit recall this rich history and speak to birthing new industries for the Clyde waterfront, imagining a future that very much looks to its past with pride.

Lavery and Cain search for attunement to the makings of the exhibit underway. Using an illusionary technique termed "Pepper's Ghost," combining plate glass and lighting effects common in theater and magic acts, things appear, disappear, and morph into one another. The technique dates back to 1866 when John Pepper first demonstrated the technique invented by Henry Dircks. Modern examples employ this device in theme parks, museums, and films. The use of this technique for his 3D unit within the installation, playing with new technologies and related software, is inspired by such inventive thinking as they seek ways to respond to the ideas and forms developing across all artists. Layers or dimensions of experience concerning demolition, felt loss and destruction, alongside the rebuilding of Glasgow, are accessed through imagery and text folding into a four-minute response accompanied by fitting music and poetry.

Galloway and Cain's glasswork seems to float within the installation space, creating a soft, circular movement. Galloway's attraction to the creative aspects of glass and the many ways it can be formed is concretely evidenced as Cain's drawings are etched into the glass form, asking viewers to look about, through, into, and beyond, suggesting connections to the movement up and down the river of the Clyde-built ships and the newly built Riverside Museum, recalling this history.

Lawless and Cain concern themselves with material and technical relationships across printmaking and architecture. The screenprints that manifest enter the installation space quietly. In doing so, a respect for space as historical is understood. Their response to the project as a whole echoes the history of the Clyde and the primacy of process with screenprints that focus on architectural details and the ways the materials were used together on-site, such as a brace, merge, intersection, bond tether, confluence, dovetail, cladding, column, skyjack, inside wall, and plateau.

Cain (2011) describes the creative engagement among all participants as an attempt "to expose the processes between us all and show how the progression of our discoveries has been worked through" (www.patriciacain.com/index. html). Thus, the installation takes a narrative form as the story of the River Clyde and its ship-building history is told and retold from multiple viewpoints, with past infusing present, moving into a future with a growing cognizance of its embedded temporality, contingencies, and potentiality. A search for narrative unity infuses the installation experience as I immerse myself within the tales told and being retold, creating my own telling tale.

The exhibit's—*Drawings (on) Riverside*—embrace of its conversational design, inquiry-guided organization, and narrative form, stem from valuing its relational workings underway and ensuing. Acknowledgment of what each artist and their particular interpretations bring to the installation is a given. The genesis of the installation demands receptivity to these givens and the artists' engagement that evolves. Willingness to embrace the associated contingencies encountered through process is integral to acting on the disclosures revealed as productive and catalytic to the making movement itself. The installation's relational inter- sections of time, place, and identities denote attunement to process, illuminating the regeneration of the Clyde riverside and its maritime heritage. I, too, bring my relations to bear, and this is of course what the installation calls for and thrives on, as more and more participants generate the relational makings and resulting understandings, positioning all involved as makers of meaning.

Dewey's "Texture in the Actual"

The contributing artists' (Cain, Nisbet, Lavery, Galloway, and Lawless) capaci- ties to attend to the creating process of meaning-making from within the process itself is characterized by Dewey (1934) as imaginative vision. It is this capacity to see what is already at play and cultivate potential elicited through "the possibilities that are interwoven within the texture of the actual" (p. 345) that attunement to process demands. Dewey (1916) clearly articulates such attunement to process as constituting thinking, revealing its method within an educative experience (p. 163). In understanding educative experiences to be located at the intersections of situation and interaction, he clarifies that it is their inseparability derived from the particularities of situation and interaction that gives each experience a unique structure. The undergirding unity and move- ment are critical to Dewey's (1938) notion of experience as a movement of thinking. Both Dewey (1934) and Cain (2011) explore the function and nature of this movement. Through putting their thinking in conversation with each other, the ensuing texture reveals telling significances.

Dewey (1916) discusses the unity of subject matter with method and the absurdity of distinguishing each from the other. He states: "Never is method outside of material" (p. 165). The exhibit, *Drawing (on) Riverside*, is alive with the relational complexities across artists, and their interpretations alongside the specifics of context, history, and personal experience become the materials of method. Constructed on-site, the experience of the exhibit is "not a combination of mind and world, subject and object, method and subject matter, but is a single continuous interaction of a great diversity (literally countless in number) of energies" (Dewey, 1916, p. 167). It is the deliberative engagement with these relationships that is the indispensible condition of thinking methodologically.

Dewey (1916) further explains that it is artificial to separate self from experience. The "what" (the experience) and the "how" (the experiencing) permeate each other and form the experiential whole (pp. 168–169). This is why he refers to method as both general and particular. Its generality is determined through a repertoire of practice accumulated within situations cultivating some skill and assuredness regarding techniques, strategies, properties of materials, and features of processes. But he insists that it is only through attention to its individuality that method can locate and act on opportunities unique to given situations. Through bringing artists into a collaborative working relationship, the exhibit gives expression to the capacity to enable each individual to draw on their own powers and find their own purposes within shared action. The cross-section of artistic expertise, techniques, and media offers a familiar place to begin for each artist. But as the exhibit takes shape, each artist finds himself or herself engaged in unexpected ways, adapting to the "exigencies" of the given particularities (Dewey, 1916, p. 171). The exhibit created is not entirely predetermined. Dewey insists that more originality and substance are attained through investing in the individual's action guided by the purposeful exploration of subject matter. The construction of the exhibit reflects this general/individual movement of thinking marked by traits that Dewey identifies as "directedness, open-mindedness, single-mindedness (or whole-heartedness), and responsibility" (p. 173). It is the investment in these traits that fosters fertile learning terrain for all involved.

Directedness

Directedness is tangible as all participating artists respond willingly to the possibilities at stake within the proposed exhibit and continue to do so as they work together "rising to the needs of the situation" (Dewey, 1916, p. 174). Confidence is the descriptor Dewey gives to this trait, understood not as self-confidence but as a confidence in process or "faith in the possibilities of the situation" (p. 174).

Open-mindedness

Open-mindedness is the necessary vigilance Dewey (1916) claims ought to accompany interest to keep ensuring growth and challenge through questioning one's assumptions and perceptions. Dewey states: "Intellectual growth means constant expansion of horizons and consequent formation of new purposes and new responses" (p. 175). The exhibit positions those that partake in the experience to have this attitude of mind as multiple perspectives and narratives of experience complicate, expand, and transform understandings. The exhibit invites "a kind of passivity, willingness to let experiences accumulate and sink in and ripen" that fosters the imaginative and physical space hospitable to open-mindedness (p. 176).

Single-mindedness

Single-mindedness is described by Dewey (1916) as nurtured through absorption, engrossment, and full concern with subject matter for its own sake manifesting the mental integrity of sincere, active response (p. 176). The artists' genuine interest is immediately palatable in the exhibit and positions the viewer to take an interest and follow the path that interest reveals.

Responsibility

Personal response entails responsibility, according to Dewey (1916). It assumes cognizance of what one is orienting toward, alongside why, how, when, and where, "acknowledging them within action" (p. 178). Such mindfulness permeates the nature of responsibility, asking all who respond accordingly to continually discern what is at stake in any situation and ascertain the proper response given the particularities involved. A unity of purpose infuses such responsible enactment and the exhibit expresses such co-commitment.

"Intellectual Hospitality"

Dewey (1916) is clear that the nature of method outlined above as being always in the making is critical to teachers' perceptions alongside their pedagogical conduct, and also directly applicable to students' perceptions alongside their pursuit of learning. *Drawings (on) Riverside* is a living example of attention to the conditions and structures that cultivate such participatory engagement. There is an experienced integrity that envelops viewers, bringing them near to the artists' individual and collective thinking and encouraging viewers to enter and partake in the conversation underway. Every viewer can enter into the conversation: there is not a readiness pre-test; there is not a mastery-level entrance requirement; nor a set way to proceed through the exhibit. Rather, very different assumptions undergird participation. Multiplicity is valued and encouraged. Becoming a part of a larger conversation is interdependent with seeking multiplicities of all kinds and assumes an ongoing reciprocal relationship across self, subject matter, and method.

Dewey (1916) describes how pedagogical method has been undermined and neglected through the isolation of self, method, and subject matter. He asks:

"What do teachers imagine is happening to thought and emotion when the latter get no outlet in the things of immediate activity?" (p. 178). Encouraging the visibility of thought and emotion throughout learning experiences, Dewey insists that the way each learner engages will vary, remaining "the personal concern, approach, and attack of an individual, and no catalogue can ever exhaust their diversity of form and tint" (p. 173). The Riverside Museum exhibit does not have a catalogue that maps out the experience, imposing a unified approach. Rather, it fosters an attitude of mind that actively welcomes what each viewer brings, prompting further growth. Dewey sees that learning conceived as such is always in motion, seeking new purposes and expanded ways of responding. Dewey's comment that comparing abilities in relation and quality to others "is irrelevant to [a teacher's] work" (p. 172) emphasizes how individuals need to draw on their own powers as they participate and gain insights with others. He terms this attitude "intellectual hospitality" (p. 175), which orients toward the qualities found within attunement to process. Eisner's (1972) statement seems very fitting:

> What is mediated through thought are qualities, what is managed in process are qualities, and what terminates at the end is a qualitative whole; an art form that expresses something by virtue of the way in which those qualities have been created and organized.
>
> *p. 114*

It is these qualities that become the makings for action and guide its development in meaningful and hospitable ways.

"Evolution of the Practitioner"

The makings found within attunement to processes of all kinds insist on practitioner openness to the perception, selection, and responsiveness to qualities encountered through the making process. The trust placed in process embraces contingencies as expected and as being productive. Cain's (2010, 2011) drawing studies literally draw us into this trusting negotiation and the significances of these found qualities. Dewey (1904) characterizes the necessary vision to do so as demanding "internal attention" rather than "external attention." Internal attention looks to the relationships at play within situations as the terrain of learning. External attention ignores the relations at play and looks toward predetermined results and predefined ways of responding (pp. 22–23). Qualities manifesting themselves in Cain's drawing studies and the exhibit as a whole enact the creation of internal meaning. Through exploration, adaptation, and manipulation, artists and viewers seek pattern, order, and, comprehensively, meaning-making. The capacity to see and act on these qualities fosters meaning-makings' enactment and is supported by contexts instilling holistic personal investment within process. Contributing to the creation of such contexts is (1) willingness to be receptive to sensory qualities and relations, ensuring conditions for close observation and time to dwell within learning situations to locate the potential and act on it; (2) acknowledgment and valuing of multiple ways to understand and engage learning situations grounded in personal lived experience; (3) commitment fueled by what Schiller (1795) termed "inner necessities" —the active and receptive relations to the environment of the emotional, social, and physical attachments acting as an ongoing catalyst for genuine participation; (4) room to deliberate, synthesize, and internalize understandings through invention of meaning that values experimentation and speculation; and (5) dialogue and interaction serving as meaningful mediums fostering connections. The *Drawings (on) Riverside* exhibit is such a participatory context, instilling these ways of seeing, feeling, and acting, prompting further inquiry and developing and enlarging self-understandings. It offers the mediating space to negotiate meaning-making belonging to the self and situation within the evolving movement of meaning-making's own enactment. It becomes difficult to distinguish specific entities as all parts are linked in relation to the vital movement of the whole. Thus, as Dewey (1934) states, "Unity is found in the cooperative roles they [parts] play in active and receptive relations to the environment" (p. 252).

The enactive nature of practitioner knowledge is Cain's (2010) thesis, which she grounds in embodied knowledge, turning to the theorizing of Varela (1986, 1995, 1997). Akin to Varela's concern for embodied knowledge, Cain explains how her drawing "is concerned with discovering what can be known through the experience of making" (p. 267). Dewey (1934) terms this *drawing out*, in search of what the subject matter has to say in particular to each of us, given our own experiences (p. 92). It is these enactive characterizations that inform how I think of teachers' evolving practitioner knowledge. Such knowledge assumes a teaching stance that is "inquiry oriented" (Cochran-Smith & Lytle, 2009), building relationships among self, students, subject matter, and contexts. Thayer-Bacon (2004) explains that such "a relational approach to education insists that [teachers] must focus on the process of learning and consider very deeply how we can help students, as social beings in relations with others, become knowers" (p. 168). The curricular undertaking, then, is to attend to the relational giveness of all educative situations. Thus, the simultaneousness of the interplay of relations continually forms the curricular space for constructing and reconstructing understandings.

Curricular enactment that sees and acts on the primacy of relations is interdependent with a teaching capacity to be in touch, mindful within the processes of actual teaching/learning experiences. Dewey (1938) claims such mindfulness places teachers at the vortex of inquiry, actively seeking connections with students, cognizant of two matters:

> First that the problem grows out of the conditions of the experience being had in the present, and that it is within the range of the capacity of students;

and secondly, that is such that it arouses in the learner an active quest for information and of production of new ideas.

p. 79

Curricular enactment conceived as such is inventive and responsive. As teachers surrender to this inventive and responsive curricular movement, it becomes a medium that asks teachers to think within its accordances and limitations (Eisner, 1998). In so doing, teachers become absorbed in relations that cannot be reduced to a set of applied rules. Judgments are made throughout process, derived from a rightness deemed fitting. Within the makings and doings, curricular enactment gains substance and takes shape. It is through such shaping that teachers enact theory/practice as simultaneous relationships reframing the nature and responsibilities of practitioner knowledge.

Historically, teacher education and professional development have grappled with the relation of theory to practice and practice to theory (see, for example, Dewey, 1904). Currently, teacher education and professional development models world-wide continue to grapple with linking the visions offered by theories with teaching and learning practices (see, for example, Cochran-Smith & Lytle, 2009; Cochran-Smith, Feiman-Nemser, McIntyre, & Demers, 2008; Darling-Hammond, 2006; Fullan, 2007; Groundwater-Smith & Mockler, 2009; Kemmis & Smith, 2008; Korthagen, 2001). An overview of the historical and current educational research literature suggests that theory and practice is typically understood as a transfer problem, with the traditional "application-of-theory model" persisting, despite little empirical evidence of improved teaching practices and student achievement.

Thus, the basic question of how to integrate theory and practice is a persistent one. For example, the roles of reflection within teachers' practices as attempts to bridge the theory/practice transfer problem in teacher education and ongoing professional development has dominated the research literature over the last 30 years. Strategies for promoting reflection and their effects are well documented. So, reflection continues to be identified as an important medium for negotiating theory/practice relationships, but its relation to improved teaching and learning remains ambiguous (see, for example, Brookfield, 1995; Dewey, 1904; Griffiths, 2000; Korthagen & Vasalos, 2005; Schon, 1987, 1995; Simpson, Jackson, & Aycock, 2005; Zeichner & Liston, 1996).

The formulation of Professional Development Schools (PDS) and their roles toward bridging the theory/practice transfer problem in teacher education and modeling professional development provide another example, also dominating the research literature. These efforts reflect an emphasis on grounding theories in professional contexts, with professional development increasingly conceptualized as an ongoing reflective interaction between theoretical notions and personal practices. Although PDS projects document some success regarding the integration of theory and practice (see, for example, Borko, 2004; Garet,

Birman, Porter, Desimone, & Suk Yoon, 2001), studies also illustrate problems (see, for example, Bullough & Baughman, 1997; Warren Little, 2002). Castle (1997) concludes that "many of the problems stem from the reality that change of this nature involves individuals and relationships" (p. 221) and the individual teacher's role has been disregarded. As Hargreaves (2002) and Day (2004) note, reformers have not always valued teachers and their impact on classroom practices.

Recently (2010), the National Council for Accreditation of Teacher Education (NCATE), to improve student learning, called for teacher education to be grounded within clinical practice across the United States. Acknowledging that some PDS initiatives and other related teacher education initiatives are meeting with some success, the much wider concern for cultivating teachers attentive to the development of learning is identified as a priority. The centrality of practitioner knowledge is foregrounded. The necessity of developing close working relationships across schools, teacher preparation programs, and all involved, is considered to be critical to the future of teacher preparation. These considerations are reiterated in the research literature world-wide (e.g., Cochran-Smith et al., 2008; Day, 2004; Dunne & Hogan, 2004; Groundwater-Smith & Mockler, 2009; Hansen, 2011; Kemmis & Smith, 2008; Loughran, 2006, 2010; Macintyre Latta & Wunder, 2012; Phelan & Sumsion, 2008; Pinar, 2003; Taubman, 2009; Winston, 2010).

All the above examples reveal that at the crux of the attempts to bridge theory and practice through reflection, PDS, and as negotiated within clinical practice, are interdependent questions regarding the nature of practitioner knowledge and the necessary conditions for the development of practitioner knowledge. Acknowledging that the research literature reflects significant growth in understandings of knowledge, basic questions about the nature of teachers' knowledge still remain (see, for example, Cochran-Smith et al., 2008). Munby, Russell, and Martin (2001) state that the nature and development of that knowledge is only beginning to be understood by the present generation of researchers in teaching and teacher education. Many current educational researchers concur, establishing the complexity of practitioner knowledge (see, for example, Cochran-Smith, 2003; Darling-Hammond, 2006; Groundwater-Smith & Mockler, 2009; Kemmis & Smith, 2008; Korthagen, 2001; Labaree, 2000; Schuck & Russell, 2005). It seems the process element in professional development has been neglected.

Clearly, for some time now, the problem that theory does not necessarily follow into practice has been heralded. As a teacher educator working alongside practicing and prospective teachers, I see much affirmation of this problematic theory/practice chasm. Theory is forgotten or deformed (Macintyre Latta, 2004), teaching opportunities fostering meaningful action for learners and learning are curtailed (Hostetler, 2011; Hostetler, Macintyre Latta, & Sarroub, 2007), and awareness of the lived terms and conditions for acting on theory are estranged

(Macintyre Latta, Buck, Leslie-Pelecky, & Carpenter, 2007). So I return over and over again to the simultaneous nature of theory/practice relations and the needed responsible enactment characterizing practitioner knowledge.

The "enactive evolution of the practitioner" (Cain, 2010) invests in the formative nature of knowledge. Practitioners must live the formative language of such practice through "encountering, negotiating, studying, and articulating the relational complexities of their classrooms" (Macintyre Latta & Wunder, 2012, p. 10). Gaining access to and responding to given relational complexities is the deliberative theory/practice terrain worthy of practitioners and their students. This is the deliberative terrain Cain *draws out* through attunement to the process of drawing, again and again. Hansen (2005) explains that such attunement to process within any educative situation points "to what the teacher is capable of deriving or drawing from it" (p. 58). Moving accordingly constitutes practitioner knowledge rising to the needs of each curricular situation with "attentive care ... devoted to the conditions which give each present experience a worthwhile meaning" (Dewey, 1938, p. 49). According to Dewey (1943), the development of such responsible attention instills agency in all involved through personal interest, insight, and power (p. 149).

There is little doubt that genuine attention to the enactive nature and role of practitioner knowledge is long overdue in education. Dire consequences have been noted for some time. Dewey (1902) identifies them as *evils* that include the lack of organic learning connections resulting in *dead*, *barren*, and limited understandings, the lack of internal motivation through mechanical instruction resulting in rote responses, and the lack of reliance on genuine interest with subject matter "presented as stuff only for memory," resulting in meaningless activities (pp. 202–204). But, as Dewey (1902) poignantly remarks:

> Activities may get agreeable if long enough persisted in. It is possible for the mind to develop interest in a routine or mechanical procedure if conditions are continually supplied which demand that mode of operation and preclude any other sort.
>
> *p. 206*

Rather, Dewey (1938) insists attunement to process emphasizes that:

> Whatever the level of experience, we have no choice but either to operate in accord with the pattern it provides or else neglect the place of intelligence in the development and control of a living and moving experience.
>
> *p. 88*

Drawings (on) Riverside embodies that thing we call the "curriculum," understood as a living and moving experience attuned to process. In such curricular enactment, "the teacher knows neither what the present power, capacity, or attitude is, nor yet how it is to be asserted, exercised, and realized," but assumes that it is the learners' "present powers which are to assert themselves," the learners' "present capacities which are to be exercised," and the learners' "present attitudes which are to be realized" (Dewey, 1902, p. 209).

Valuing interests, insights, and the enactive powers harbored within them holds wisdom for teaching (and practices of all kinds) worth drawing everyone's attention toward. Cain's (2011) exhibit, *Drawings (on) Riverside*, reminds me of the artist within all curricular makers, as given relations are trusted to form the curricular ground, offer the curricular materials of method, prompt deliberation alongside attunement to process, and suggest curricular enactment that is not entirely predicted. In these ways, curricular enactment orients toward meaning-making processes inciting dialogue, negotiation, and interaction that are alive with creative tensions that practitioner knowledge must live and speak within (Jardine, 1992, p. 126), telling a tale with significances for all involved. It is a tale that trusts process. It is a tale that entrusts teachers and their students with enactive curricular responsibilities. And, it is a tale that can no longer be distrusted. After all, it is a tale where mistrust has led to vastly underestimated curricular consequences and costs for teachers, teaching, learners, and learning.

9

FOSTERING SELF-UNDERSTANDINGS IN RELATION TO WIDER CONTEXTS AND CITIZENRY

FIGURE 9.1 *Ambush in the Leaf #4*, Chlorophyll Print and Resin, Binh Dahn, 2007.

The great thing for one as for the other is ... education which enables him [*sic*] to see within his [*sic*] daily work all there is in it of large and human significance.

Dewey, 1943, p. 24

Binh Danh is a contemporary photographer and teacher concerned with memorializing memories (see http://binhdanh.com/projects.html). His exhibit, *Viet Nam, Nebraska* (2011–2012) held at the Sheldon Museum of Art,[6] University of Nebraska-Lincoln, United States, continues his lifelong exploration of memory. As a Vietnamese refugee he arrived in the United States in 1979 as a two-year-old from a Malaysian camp. His family—a mother, father, and siblings—were "boat people" who fled Vietnam because of harsh conditions following what Americans know as the Vietnam War and Vietnamese term the American War. Danh relays how his parents did not talk about Vietnam, the war, or their journey to California as he grew up. It was through photographs that he began to access his family's history. He finally gained some sense of his father's scars, a constant memory for his father of fighting alongside the Americans in the war. Images of family life, cultural roots, and Buddhist spiritual beliefs and practices reconstructed Danh's history. He increasingly associated what it meant to be alive as connected to his contemplations since childhood of all living things being composed of atoms, continually cycling into new forms. Time, decay, and regeneration are understood as being elemental to life and interrelated with living. Thus, Danh came to understand human memory as intimately linked with the earth's memory, and his artworks convey this interest and document the ensuing paths of exploration.

Danh (2011) explains that connections within and across our personal and collective memories surface embodied matters that he grapples with as his images convey the struggle of memory with remembering and forgetting. He understands memory constituting our very beings and sees his photography confronting and re-membering these images of selves in the world (artist lecture, September 23, 2011, Sheldon Museum of Art, University of Nebraska-Lincoln). Thus, memory is entangled with temporality, and as Bal (2002) points out, entails mediation (p. 182). She explains that "memory turns out to be multilayered, overdetermined, disunified, and emphatically cultural," soliciting "memory without foreclosing the past it acts upon" (p. 185). It is such a mediating space, or what Gadamer (2000) terms a "clearing" (p. 257), that Danh's images invite and come upon.

Clearings

A clearing exists beyond "our wanting and doing" (Gadamer, 2000, p. xxviii). Danh's images, forming the *Viet Nam, Nebraska* exhibit (see www.sheldonartmuseum.org/exhibitions/past_exhibitions.html), call us into such clearings. I approach each image cognizant that I am coming upon something that already is, beyond my "wanting and doing"—thus, given. This is the nature of mediation within memorialization. Memory is thus formative, incomplete, and, as Gadamer (2000) insists, integral to humanity's finite historical being. He states: "In a way that has long been insufficiently noticed, forgetting is closely related to keeping in mind and remembering" (p. 16). It is through forgetting that clearings offer opportunities to see anew. And so each clearing instills a reverence for what is given, positioning those that enter the clearings to respond with respect or awe for what is there (Garrison & Rud, 2009). I am one of many people coming upon the *Viet Nam, Nebraska* exhibit, and I attend with reverence to my path into, within, and beyond the clearings. I also attend to the paths of others into, within, and beyond the clearings. These paths share the experiential stance of both self-forgetfulness and of mediation with self (Gadamer, 2000, p. 128). Indeed, the clearings for one and for the other hold what Dewey (1943) terms a "great thing" to see within these works, "all there is in it of large and human significance" (p. 24). Memorialization is solicited. Dewey (1934) clarifies, "art ... renders men [*sic*] aware of their union with one another in origin and destiny" (p. 271).

My path into the clearings offered by the *Viet Nam, Nebraska* exhibit confronts much new terrain. As I come upon each image I learn that Danh has a particular interest in the relationships to the land that connects people to place. In particular, Danh finds himself compelled by peoples displaced from their homelands. The images comprising the exhibit foreground some of the personal and collective stories of the Vietnamese community in Lincoln, Nebraska. The exhibit's opening brings the local Vietnamese community to the Sheldon Museum of Art. Pride alongside a deep respect for the personal stories present in each image exudes from the Vietnamese community within the context created by the exhibit. Danh's collected memories of Vietnamese Americans living in Lincoln form a portrait of the community as individuals negotiate a place for themselves and their families.

My own ignorance is confronted as I acknowledge I know very little about the Vietnamese community in Lincoln and throughout Nebraska. I learn that it is estimated that 6,943 Vietnamese currently live in Nebraska (Nebraska Census Data, 2010). As Lincoln, a city with a current population of approximately 300,000, became a resettlement area for immigrants from over 40 countries over the last three decades, immigration through refugee populations began to dramatically increase. As someone transplanted to Lincoln myself, I first looked at a map of the United States to see where I was heading. Lincoln is in the very center of the country and is often referred to as "the middle of nowhere." But, as Pipher (2002) points out in her book, *The Middle of Everywhere: The World's Refugees Come to Our Town*, Lincoln swiftly became a gathering place for refugees and immigrants from all over the world. Lincoln is the nation's eighteenth largest resettlement area for Asian refugees and immigrants. Nebraska is the fifth state in refugee resettlement per capita when compared with states of similar population. A relatively low cost of living with access to jobs and a high number of social service agencies, churches, and additional support services makes Lincoln an attractive resettlement destination.

The fall of Saigon (now called Ho Chi Minh City) in 1975 and the end of the war in Vietnam precipitated the Vietnamese arrival in Lincoln during the late 1970s and early 1980s. Under the Indochina Migration and Refugee Assistance Act passed on May 23, 1975, approximately 130,000 refugees from South Vietnam, Laos, and Cambodia entered the United States under a special status and with some relocation and financial aid. The Refugee Act further reduced restrictions on entry, while the Vietnamese government established the Orderly Departure Program under the United Nations High Commissioner for Refugees in response to world outcry—allowing people to leave Vietnam legally for family reunions and for humanitarian reasons. Additional American laws were passed, allowing children of American servicemen and former political prisoners and their families to enter the United States. Another peak of Vietnamese immigrants to the United States was in 1992, when many former military officers and government workers from the former regime of South Vietnam, who had been held in prison camps termed "reeducation camps" operated by the government following the end of the Vietnam War, were released or sponsored by their families to come to the United States. Between 1981 and 2000, the United States accepted 531,310 Vietnamese political refugees and immigrants.

This overview marks some of the historical accountings, but of course it is the personal lived accounts that bear "the body's imprint" (Bowman, 2004, p. 46). Danh (2011) terms such imprinting "the transcendent condition of memory," superseding any written histories as he prints images of the war's dead on plant leaves and other organic materials. Bodily memories are evoked as personal memories become entangled within the earth's stories of past, present, and future. These images are powerful, reaching beyond themselves and positioning viewers to consider the human toll of the Vietnam War and all wars. I wonder about the return of these long-forgotten faces reflecting back at me as artifacts of a history I know little about. I wonder about the memories elicited for others. Archival footage as part of a video installation reveals some sense of the precariousness of the boat people's journeys and some access to the human desperation permeating these lived accounts. These images have a residual effect on me, as I perceive all of the remaining images of the exhibit with some sense of the burdensome history and its associated painful memories. The exhibit's additional images tell of lives today through the Asian markets and restaurants, the Vietnamese Catholic church, the Buddhist Temple, and the growing families and their home lives, as Vietnamese refugees and immigrants make a place for themselves in Lincoln, Nebraska. Danh's intent is to give the Vietnamese community representation within Lincoln. Family photographs gathered from the community documenting their time in Nebraska fill two wall-sized installation pieces. The images prompt me to want to know more about the imagery bound within each photograph. I have many questions about the Vietnamese community in Lincoln, Nebraska that I did not know I even had. I turn to individuals from the Vietnamese community to attend to their distinct responses as I walk alongside some of them into the clearings offered by the exhibit.[7]

Phuong

Phuong has recently arrived from Vietnam to study at the University of Nebraska-Lincoln. She has come to Lincoln with her husband and child and has now been here for about eight weeks. Phuong tells me that when I mentioned the exhibit to her that she became genuinely excited to attend. She explains she has felt at a loss, displaced—missing the familiarity of her country, her home, her family and friends. The exhibit is an opportunity to connect and she takes much pride in talking with me about these personal connections. Phuong frankly tells me, though, that the images and stories of the boat people are quite new to her. She questions why she does not know these stories. She recalls little knowledge of these accounts from her childhood and schooling. Phuong does come from a town where the toxic after-effects of Agent Orange, a code name for a herbicide used during the Vietnam War by the US military as a means to defoliate forested and rural land, are quite evident. She describes with much sadness the children affected by Agent Orange in her town, who are deformed and incapacitated, but concomitantly confronts her lack of understanding concerning the historical and political tensions undergirding the war in her country. But she has wondered about these happenings and talks about her attempts to expand her understandings through following up on her questions through personal inquiries. Phuong tells me that she found herself moved to tears as the artist, Binh Danh, talked of his return as an adult accompanied by his mother to the camp in Malaysia where his family had found refuge, and to Vietnam and their work with a community of children suffering the effects of Agent Orange. Phuong states: "I was deeply touched by his forgiveness and his need to return to his birthplace and retrace some of the family's journey. I was struck by his concern and I felt his deep attachment to place" (personal communication, October 7, 2011).

Anthony

Anthony has just graduated from the University of Nebraska-Lincoln. He came to the United States from Vietnam in 1994, when he was six years old, with his parents and two older brothers. His father had been held in a reeducation camp from 1975 till 1981, but the family did not leave Vietnam right away upon his release. It was through the efforts of the Vietnamese in the United States that prisoners once held in these camps could come to the United States, sponsored by their families. Anthony's family saved for their journey for a number of years. They arrived in Hawaii initially, but found jobs and support in Lincoln, Nebraska. Anthony's gaze as he moves through the exhibit seems most interested in the archival footage of the boat people. Anthony tells me he knows some of these stories through the Vietnamese community and the images make some of these lived accounts very vivid. He tells me he does not know much about his father's experience in the reeducation camp and how his family has focused their efforts on investing in their new life ever since their decision to immigrate to the United States. Anthony actually finds that he does not see much of himself in the exhibit, commenting, "I obviously recognize local places and some of the people but I do not see much evidence of what young people are doing and offering. I guess I am saying I do not feel much energy or vitality" (personal communication, October 11, 2011). Anthony's tone and words convey purposefulness within his life that seems keenly aware of a responsibility to family and friends. Anthony also wonders why his Christian Vietnamese church community is not depicted while other images reference the Catholic and Buddhist communities. Our path into the exhibit concludes with Anthony stating:

> I am very much a part of the Vietnamese community in Lincoln but I am also very much a part of the community at large. I do feel and see some connections, but I think there are more … it does not seem complete … or maybe, it is what is missing, what I do not know, that I feel uneasy about.
>
> *Personal communication, October 11, 2011*

Uyen

Uyen is a senior at the University of Nebraska-Lincoln. She is eager to tell me about the pride and courage of her father, a second lieutenant during the Vietnam War. Uyen is particularly moved by the images of dead soldiers on the leaves as we begin to explore the exhibit. She has read about the process used by the artist and explains it to me, articulating how the care and time taken by the artist to produce these daguerreotype images seems so fitting for the personal costs of lives lost and how these losses are still felt in so many ways today. Uyen tells me the unknown stories underneath each of the printed leaves speak to her in important ways. She motions toward the video footage of the boat people and she quickly tells me she knows many of these accounts and how these accounts resonate very deeply with her as well. Uyen did not come to the United States as a boat person. Her father spent five years in a reeducation camp and upon his release the decision was made to make arrangements for the family to move. But her mother passed away from cancer just prior to their journey, so Uyen's father, accompanied by his then three-year-old daughter, boarded the plane together. The close bond between father and daughter is felt in Uyen's words and expressions. Uyen's father has shared with her some of the brutality and disrespect he experienced in the camps. Uyen also explains that she knows many of the traditional Vietnamese songs and wartime tunes as they were a large part of her early years as her father shared these with her. Uyen voices her strong commitment to remixing these songs and sharing them with youth today as a means for communicating the underlying stories, so these accounts do not become lost or forgotten. She tells me she purchased the exhibit catalogue of the Vietnamese soldiers for her father. Uyen's father keeps in touch with other soldiers from the reeducation camps and recently traveled to San Jose for a reunion with some of them. Uyen drove with her father on this trip and she tells me the event organizers honored them for their commitment to driving so far to attend. The loyalty she describes to her father, to her Vietnamese culture, and her history, comes through passionately. Uyen tells me, "My Dad and I sewed a Republican flag so we could use it for school and social events … if I was participating in an event or team sport, I always took the flag with me … my dad insisted that it always be displayed" (personal communication, October 18, 2011). She proudly points out the large flag in the exhibit as a reference for me. She also proudly tells me that the image in the exhibit of the new plaza under construction with Vietnamese businesses is exciting. Our conversation comes to a close with Uyen emphasizing to me that she purposefully invests in educative opportunities on campus to promote Vietnamese culture and history. She notes her active involvement in the student-led Asian World Alliance on campus (personal communication, October 18, 2011).

"The Individual and the World": Play of "Roots and Routes"

There is much of Dewey's (1916) thinking in his chapter "The individual and the world," in his book *Democracy and Education* that fittingly surfaces as the individual paths taken into the clearings of the Viet Nam exhibit unfold. Dewey articulates how dualistic interpretations separate the individual mind from the world, denying the agency of knowledge. He reframes individuality away from understandings of self-sufficiency and independence as reliant on a self "building up knowledge anew on its own account" (p. 295) toward the "development of agencies for revising and transforming previously accepted beliefs" (p. 305). It is this agentic power within human beings' capacity for reorganization (p. 294) that is prompted through the Viet Nam exhibit. All who come upon and enter the clearings afforded by the exhibit are positioned to enter with "inquiring, hunting, searching attitude, instead of one of mastery and possession" (p. 295). The exhibit as a whole incites the thinking Dewey envisions as revising and transforming an individual's knowledge as convictions are reorganized. This reorganizing thinking movement is marked by "factors" identified by Dewey (1910) as forming and informing each other on the paths into, within, and beyond the clearings, that more typically work against each other. It is the act of achieving what Dewey (1910) terms "balance" (p. 214) or Kant (1790) terms "concert" (p. 71) within the forming and reforming of reorganization that compels my attention as I attend to the paths of Phuong, Anthony, and Uyen into the clearings of the exhibit marked by negotiating Dewey's factors within thinking of "the unconscious and the conscious," "process and product," and "the far and the near" (pp. 214–224).

Dewey (1910) claims a rhythmic movement of the unconscious and conscious is entailed in all "fruitful thinking" (p. 215). Unconscious assumptions, values, and beliefs made explicit birth opportunities to see anew. In doing so, "spontaneity" and "freshness" are elicited alongside "conviction" and "control" (p. 219). In the lived experiences conveyed by Phuong, Anthony, and Uyen, I hear a shared pride in their Vietnamese heritage, but I also hear different personal values, assumptions, and beliefs concerning this heritage derived from varied life experiences. As these unconscious self-understandings are made explicit and gain greater self-consciousness, the visibility warrants self-scrutiny. The "original difficulty" (Dewey, 1910, p. 215) of the nature of understandings becomes increasingly tangible as I attend to more and more perspectives and my own understandings are brought to bear.

Dewey (1910) claims this rhythmic movement of thinking infuses process and product, instilling the "attitude of the artist" in self and others (p. 220). Such an attitude values the journeys into, within, and beyond the clearings provided by the Viet Nam exhibit and trusts that process will shape the product en-route. The conversations with Phuong, Anthony, and Uyen reveal such interdependencies as the process of thinking itself actively shapes each of their thinking. Thus, thought not only shapes its products, it is constitutive of them. It is the attitude of the artist that makes rooms for this ongoing creating and inventing movement that Schiller (1795) characterizes as "energizing" and "melting" (p. 83). Self-investment in this movement takes what Dewey (1910) terms "faith in the power of thought to preserve its own integrity without external supports and arbitrary restrictions" (p. 219). Phuong, Anthony, and Uyen each care very much about their connections to the Viet Nam exhibit and each is open to entering into a dialogue confronting and exploring these connections as the integral ground for learning is personally experienced as energizing and melting.

Dewey (1910) further characterizes this movement of thinking as an interplay of the far and the near. Both far and near connections are palatable in the responses of Phuong, Anthony, and Uyen as they navigate their experiences of the exhibit. Vietnam is far away in physical proximity to all, but emotional, social, contextual, and cultural familiarity varies in distance. Vietnam is near to all through associations of personal experience, embodied memories, and cultural practices, but the depth of nearness varies. The exhibit brings these varied far and near connections to the surface, but also demands that each consider what is new, unusual, and jarring. In each case, the exhibit fosters "insights into the remote, the absent, the obscure" (p. 224) as thinking far and near is enlarged and deepened through engagement with the exhibit. The interplay of the far and the near posits alternative thinking and encourages imagination, requiring speculation and conjecturing about possibilities.

The exhibit provides clearings for critical insight into "qualities-in-qualitative-relations" (Dewey, 1934, p. 312), the "factors" at play across the "conscious and the unconscious," the "process and product," and the "far and the near." Smith (2006) relays the relations as "what we know and what we do not know, what is said and what is unsaid, what is visible and also invisible" (p. xxiv). It is this relational play that ensues with self and other(s) that is navigated through the experiential whole of the exhibit. I keep seeing so much potential for cultivating learning within such relational navigations. Too often in teaching and teacher education the relational play of learning is discouraged, thwarted, or never given any chance to gain momentum. Smith explains that

> what needs to be recovered more than anything else is a broader sense of World that can free young people from the cage of subjectivity that their own more immediate environments (including class, tribe, or nation) have constructed for them.
>
> *p. 80*

The exhibit attempts to do just this, positioning each person that takes part to situate self within what is known and what is not known, said and unsaid, and visible and invisible concerning *Viet Nam, Nebraska*. Thus, Danh's (2011) overall concern for the art exhibit's attention to participants' remembering and forgetting forms the ongoing task of reorganization for individuals that come upon the clearings afforded by the exhibit, and beyond, within the world at large.

The thinking movement instilled through Dewey's (1910) relational negotiation of the conscious and unconscious, process and product, and far and near is similarly characterized by Hansen (2011) as assisting "people in moving closer and closer apart and further and further together" (p. 3). Hansen depicts the indwelling tensions at play within this movement making more visible and tangible multiplicities, differences, and their lived consequences, alongside gaining greater concrete relational understandings and appreciations. Hansen sees this movement orienting toward a cosmopolitan way of seeing and being in the world that attends to the intellectual, ethical, and aesthetic journeying that life's paths avail. He draws upon the metaphorical depiction of Kwok-bun (2005) to image forth cosmopolitanism's catalytic role with education, meaning, and transaction, who states: "Such a life conjures the possibility of roots and routes—of place and places, of the known and the new, of memory and anticipation" (p. 13). It is the possibilities arising from acknowledging participants' roots and examining their routes into the clearings that the *Viet Nam, Nebraska* exhibit foregrounds.

My horizons of understanding have definitely been enlarged. Phuong, Anthony, and Uyen reveal personal horizons of place and places, known and new, and memory and anticipation. Gadamer (2000) explains that a horizon is an individual's range of vision (p. 302). He further explains that horizons cannot be viewed from fixed and certain ground. Rather, he describes the horizon of

the present as "constantly in the process of being formed because we are continually having to test all our prejudices" (p. 306). Tensions and particularities
between the exhibit as route and one's roots are expected and necessary to continually seeking momentary balance, concert, or a "fusion of horizons" (p. 306).
It is the journeying entailed in the continuous search for fusion of horizons that
Gadamer claims embraces the problem of application embedded within all
understandings (p. 307). Hansen (2011) explicates that the horizon's reach then
seeks "what communities and individuals are in process of becoming through
the experience of reflective openness to the new fused with reflective loyalty to
the known" (p. 86). Hansen envisions such journeying "propel[ling] persons to
express, to create, a generous response to the world" (p. 120).

Cultivating a generous response to the world illuminates what it means to
inhabit the world well with others. Hansen (2011) denotes cosmopolitanism as
cultivating the capacities to do just this (p. 45). Pinar (2009) identifies the
"worldliness" that cosmopolitanism elicits through "a state of being between
the local and the global, simultaneously self-engaged and worldly-wise, cause
and consequence of a cosmopolitan education" (p. 4). Both Hansen (2011) and
Pinar (2009) position teachers as agents for instilling the habits to inhabit the
world as "kosmopolites," denoting its Greek roots.

The clearings afforded by the *Viet Nam, Nebraska* exhibit offer insights for
educators into the necessary habits for teachers and learners to inhabit the world
as kosmopolites. The curricular vision and enactment is the teacher's responsibility. And, as Hansen (2011) insists, such envisioning permeates all disciplines
and interests as its primary concern is for learner–learning connectedness mediated in relationship to other(s). Seeking such connectedness means teachers and
students must invest in creating and sustaining a movement of thinking that
belongs to the self and situation concerned. Therefore, connectedness is mindful
of the histories and particularities of individuals and situations, attending to the
moving character of the curricular circumstances in which they find themselves.
The active reorganizing on a continual basis, thus, insists on genuine concerted
action on the parts of teachers and students, oriented toward multiplicity and
purposefulness, manifested through divergent learning processes and products.
The reorganizing movement fosters learner confidence and growth, alongside
respect and value for differences of all kinds as catalysts in coming to know self
and others because individual thinking is continually sought and made visible in
relation to others. The reorganizing movement finds its own learning pace,
generated through personal involvement, questioning what is encountered as
topics open up and unfold. Thus, the reorganizing movement is concerned with
emergence and development, with interaction, deliberation, debate, prudence,
and judgments made within process as expected participatory practices. And, in
doing so, participants re-turn and re-relate to curricular circumstances with new
eyes. The clearings afforded by the Viet Nam exhibit uncover and re-present
self-understandings, concomitantly entailing forgetting alongside mediating, thus

expanding personal and collective horizons. In other words, the reorganizing movement remembers all involved.

Myself, Phuong, Anthony, and Uyen experience remembering through the clearings of the *Viet Nam, Nebraska* exhibit as being "not an affair of coming directly into the presence of the *really real* once and for all" but growing knowledge "with the varying circumstances as we become more sensitive to the possibilities that can be realized in the varying circumstances in which we and whatever it is we are trying to understand are placed" (Boisvert, 1998, p. 25). Dewey (1916) argues that "such knowledge never can be learned by itself; it is not information, but a mode of intellectual practice, a habitual disposition of the mind" (p. 188). It entails a mode of being understood as always in process. Dewey further explains that it is within the "affections" and "aversions" of process that connections are made (p. 188). And, it seems the affections and aversions located within the reorganizing movement of the clearings offered by the Viet Nam exhibit are inseparably bound up with the question of what it means to be alive, "seeing large and human significance" (Dewey, 1943, p. 24). Such cosmopolitanism cultivates "naiveté" (Dewey, 1958, p. 21) that Granger (2006) unpacks as the necessary openness "investigating our intellectual habits through a receptivity and sense of responsibility toward formerly neglected aspects of our experiential landscape" (p. 23). Clearings, understood as the act or process of making or becoming clear, calls upon teachers' receptiveness and the associated responsibilities to keep re-envisioning their curricular experiences toward acknowledging "our common interests, illuminated through others yet accepting of otherness, in the objects and events of our protean commonplace world—our common wealth" (Granger, 2006, p. 275). It is this wealth that must be made accessible. Hansen (2011) talks of curriculum as "cosmopolitan inheritance," holding the wealth. Accessing it entails active engagement with the thinking of others, traversing the unconscious and conscious, the process and product, and the far and near, considering the local in relation to the global. Dewey (1938) places teachers at the vortex of this movement, actively fostering learning connections with students mindful of two things:

> First that the problem grows out of the conditions of the experience being had in the present, and that it is within the range of the capacity of students; and secondly, that is such that it arouses in the learner an active quest for information and of production of new ideas.
>
> *p. 79*

Dewey asks teachers to mindfully consider how they and their students inhabit learning situations as the wealth in classrooms is seen and acted upon, bridging connections both small and large. Hansen explains that through such heightened mindfulness teachers "become more fully in and of the world" (p. 46), positioning all involved to respond rather than react, and emphasizing the dynamic role of teachers within curricular enactment.

Self-understandings are always being shaped, then, in relation to varied contexts. O'Loughlin (2006) explains that it is only through such concrete practice that the necessary knowledge is embodied in lived understandings for the negotiation of social life and its associated concerns (pp. 155–156). She calls this the "actual practice of citizenship" (p. 157) and, along with Dewey (1916), sees education as a primary practice ground. Dewey calls such ground "precious" (p. 305). This is the wealth, the cosmopolitan inheritance of individual variations seen and acted upon as productive, fostering growth in self and other(s), allowing "for intellectual freedom and the play of diverse gifts and interests in its education measures" (Dewey, 1916, p. 305). Davey (2006) discloses how "unquiet understandings" manifest through encounters with the ensuing "difficulties," "distances," and "differences" (p. xiv) of "residing within the quietness of a single interpretation" (p. xvi). The *Viet Nam, Nebraska* exhibit challenges single interpretations and opens a space for exposing the play of difficulties, distances, and differences, inciting much potential for an enlarged conversation. I wonder about the possibilities that might arise by bringing Phuong, Anthony, Uyen, others, and myself into conversation together. How might the difficulties, distances, and differences intersect? How could these intersections be supported to enable enlarged understandings? The Viet Nam exhibit evidenced that all who inhabit this space "come to know what it is to become different to themselves and who realize, as a consequence, that they are indeed mutually dependent upon each other for expanding the possibilities within their understanding" (Davey, 2006, p. 12). Teachers and students need to spend more time interacting within such clearings. Gaudelli and Hewitt (2010) describe how, in their teaching/researching experiences, "such encounters can result in an awesome aesthetic that is an exemplar of what it means to be human" (p. 97). It is such precious ground that the Viet Nam exhibit clearings wander into, and in doing so, suggest curricular conditions, practices, and possibilities that make clear the role of "unquiet" understandings within seeking humanity's common wealth, and the "open, vulnerable, and in question" (Davey, 2006, p. 17) cosmopolitan inhabitants necessary for residing well within its inheritance.

10

CONCLUSION

Aesthetic Play's Clues, "Unquiet" Understandings, and the Makings of Self/World

FIGURE 10.1 *One Foggy Morning*, Alexander Macintyre, 1909.

> Children at play are ... engaged in actions that give their imagery an outward manifestation; in their play, idea and act are completely fused.
>
> *Dewey, 1934, p. 278*

From a very early age I understood and valued play as a means to make sense of my world. I recall many hours wandering outside—walking along the beach, through woodlands, up and down my street, and in my backyard. I found purpose within these ventures, and the connections instilled a trust in process and a boldness to navigate from within these experiences that very much extends into who I am today.

One incident in particular marks the self-investment within my play that Dewey (1934) describes as the complete merging of playfulness with seriousness (p. 279). I grew up on the west coast, right by the sea. In the winter months there were some foggy mornings that provided much fodder for my imaginings as I found my way to school. My Dad called it pea soup fog: "It's as thick as pea soup out there," he'd say. As I ventured from my home I encountered the wonders of a world anew, thick with magical discoveries. Unable to see more than a step ahead, my attention was drawn to the given immediacies brought by each step taken. The school building suddenly happened upon me, though my venture often mused with a building I was somehow unable to locate.

It was after one of these foggy venture-full mornings that I sat in my grade-three classroom, third row, right at the front. The teacher, Miss Moore (pseudonym), was a tall, lean, stern woman. The classroom was orderly and safe and though I would not describe Miss Moore as fun or warm, I liked her; I liked school. The classroom was silent. We were practicing cursive writing. I started diligently on the task but the letters quickly became words, and the words images; and the pea soup foggy morning meandered into a marvelous story.

I was completely absorbed in the creation of my story when Miss Moore happened upon me. She had been walking up and down the aisles and as she got to the front of the third row she glared down at my writing. She abruptly interrupted: "Margaret, this is atrocious writing! Start again!" Bewildered and startled I quickly responded, "But, Miss Moore, the ideas come out of my head so fast, I cannot possibly write them down fast enough." She curtly responded with "Stop being so cheeky. On task now!" I decided that it was an oversight on her part and continued to like her, like school—but obviously I never entirely forgave Miss Moore.

I have since recalled that incident many times as a teacher and parent. I am cognizant that teachers can incite learning, teachers can impede learning, teachers can grow learning, and teachers can halt learning. Of course, it could easily be argued that I was indeed off task. But I was learning. Miss Moore could have acknowledged my story, yet redirected me to the task at hand. But Miss Moore did not see me—a student who rarely said a thing and was almost always obedient. Miss Moore did not really hear my response nor read my story. I recall being genuinely surprised and disappointed. I confidently knew I was doing important thinking. "Idea and act" were "completely fused" (Dewey, 1934, p. 278).

Labeled a creative, imaginative child, my report cards often relayed these adjectives as distractions from learning. But my parents paid little heed to such feedback and invested in art, dance, and music lessons for me. And I knew that if indeed I had found myself unable to locate the school building on any one of those foggy mornings, my mom would have always welcomed me back whole-heartedly at home.

That incident served to map out the terrain for my life's work of understanding what teaching is or ought to entail. After all, the fog can serve as a metaphor for the play-full-work of learning. Fog created a space for deliberation, exploration, and speculation. Through deliberating, exploring, and speculating, I sought meaning. I translated these ideas—adapting, changing, and creating a story. The space generated a movement of thinking that invited and valued my participation. I recognized myself within my story; it drew on my experiences, it negotiated connections I was making, it anticipated directions I did not see coming in advance. Belongingness had been negotiated and was undeniably at stake when Miss Moore interrupted me. Seeing with potential in self, in others, in situations, is a necessity as a teacher. This entails a knowing concomitantly of past and present, with implications for the future. A teacher cannot guide learning without attending to what students bring to situations and how these relational complexities might intersect to promote learning. Teachers cannot say what students bring is not enough; nor too unfamiliar to possibly work with; nor what she/he might/might not prefer. The place to begin is amidst the fog, with what is given. And what is given ought to be seen as a gift.

I have learned most significantly about the gifts each child brings through my own children, Anna and Will. Each has taught me about difference. From their beginnings in my womb their differences were felt. One was a serious kicker, the other, a serious sleeper. At birth their needs, desires, and responses were unique and thus the relationships forged through the years are necessarily different. Alongside my partner, Bill, we marveled as new parents at how they each created and made sense of their world. I see two distinct individuals, each with wonderful strengths. Their identities are precious to me. And these precious identities are very much in the making, forming, and re-forming. I want my children to flourish, finding plentiful sustenance to feed and nurture their identities. Through Anna and Will, I gained a deep respect for Van Manen's (1991) insistence that teaching ought to show itself as "openness to children's experiences," "as subtle influence," "as holding back," "as situational confidence," "as improvisational." Teaching ought to "preserve a child's space," "save what is vulnerable," "prevent injury or hurt," "heal (make whole) what is broken," "strengthen what is good," "enhancing what is unique," sponsoring personal growth and learning. Teaching, therefore, entails "meditating through speech, through silence, through the eyes, through gesture, atmosphere, and example, giving new and unexpected shape to unanticipated situations, converting incidence into significance, never forgetting that teaching always leaves a mark on a child" (pp. 64–173).

The learning risks and opportunities afforded to each child as identities in the making are different, but the significances are similar—greater cognizance of self in relation to others and the necessity of others toward enlarging all of our understandings; instilling confidence in the processes of learning; comfort with the fog of learning ambiguity; and energized by not knowing as part of the felt difficulty/enjoyment of learning. As human beings we are all fundamentally creative. How we make sense of the world is through creating meaning. As we create meaning, we create ourselves. We negotiate our identities and we increasingly understand that this is a lifelong undertaking. When we remove these undergoings and doings of learning processes, we rob students and teachers of locating their own identities within the fog.

The attention to process required of all students of the work of learning positions learners as creators of meaning. Within the ensuing undergoings and doings of creating meaning awaits the powerful and empowering learning consequences that matter—now, and for the future. The ensuing costs of not doing so have been vastly underestimated. So, my continued efforts and hopes are for educators to claim the creative space of classrooms; creating meaning, creating self—adapting, changing, building meaning with students as co-creators. This is the needed play-space, embracing teaching with life, for the well-being of individuals and our future.

Clues

The book as a whole ventures into play-space, disclosing how play holds the "clues" to human beings' reciprocity with other(s), with the world. Play occurs "in-between," within the space that opens between self and other(s) (Gadamer, 2000, p. 111). Artworks throughout this book provide such openings to access how play "works" this space (Davey, 2006, p. 64). Every chapter depicts the being of a work of art as akin to the nature of play. As Dewey (1934) explains, there is immediacy in play, but also temporal mediation of the past brought to bear on the present, holding implications for the future. He characterizes the necessary attitude as "playful," assuming commitment and interest in finding purpose from within a learning experience (p. 279). The medium of expression gained is the "work" of art. Dewey emphasizes the interdependency of play and work. Play offers freedom from preconceived results, enabling the workings to be located, explored, and fittingly ordered into meaningful forms. It is this very act of play that both Dewey and Gadamer denote as movement; a playful experience in which human subjects lose themselves and find themselves, again and again. This playful movement is also like being in conversation for Gadamer. The inner workings of Pinar's (2010) "complicated curricular conversations" demand such playful movement. My childhood narrative of a foggy morning relays the total absorption. The narrative depicts a conversation in which the play I was absorbed within guides how the story and self unfolds. The findings, on my venture that foggy morning, form the details, the complexities that inform my journey. Following similar entrails became the work of each chapter, seeking the clues embedded within each artwork. Collectively, the character of aesthetic experience manifests. Attending to the creation of meaning from within the meaning-making experience is the aesthetic play embraced throughout. Specific features of such play emerge, suggesting clues, transforming and structuring unique learning experiences. It is this transformation which makes play educational. To still the movement would be "mis-educative" (Dewey, 1938, p. 25).

Dewey (1938) is clear that not all experience is educative. Over and over again, Dewey's concern for educative experiences is betrayed in educational policies and practices currently and throughout much of the past. Dewey (1929) puts the blame on the model of spectatorship in which a spectator views a fin-ished picture, rather than from the perspective of the artist producing the picture (p. 23). Educative experiences value the movement of thinking of the artist (learner) at work. Mis-educative experiences do not value participatory thinking. Considering this dichotomy raises and confronts the question of what constitutes experience. Each chapter in this book brings the reader near to the workings at play within educative experiences. The betrayals of educative experiences fear these workings. And these betrayals become uncomplicated curricular conversations that model spectatorship.

"Unquiet" Understandings

Dewey's (1929) concerns with the spectator model persists. Davey (2006) sim-ilarly describes human beings' fascination with "the will to method." He points out how such fascination leads to nihilistic tendencies, colonizing and dehu-manizing human experience of all kinds (pp. 20–22) that speaks to the costs of betraying Dewey's educative experience to me. Aesthetic play is portrayed throughout this book as fostering Davey's "unquiet" understandings that trouble the will to method and prompt educative experiences. Davey describes how nihilistic tendencies separate subjects from their objects and from their world, and apply preconceived frameworks to situations that ensure certainty and valid-ity. Aesthetic play depends on uncertainties, and its validity is determined on an ongoing basis as attunement within situations is sought. Meaningfulness is pursued, valuing the participatory act of doing so. Nihilistic tendencies thwart this movement of aesthetic play. The subject is blinded to the inner working of situations and assumes control over the situation. The result, as Davey (drawing on Gadamer's [2000], insights) explains, "promotes an alienated form of knowing that not only distances the subject from the subject matter that shape its sensibility but which also renders it increasingly deaf to their address" (2006, p. 21). Csordes (1994) explains how the differing orientations result in primary concern with preconceived representations of experience or primary commit-ment within lived experiences: "Representation is fundamentally nominal, and hence we can speak of a representation. Being-in-the-world is fundamentally conditional, and hence we can speak of existence and lived experience" (p. 10). Thus, representation values the will to method's nihilistic tendencies rather than the experiential terrain of being-in-the-world. It is representation's pull that alienates knowledge away from subject matter, suppressing subjectivity and its inherent agency and vitality to be awakened through aesthetic play.

Davey (2006) further describes how the will to method holds colonizing tendencies that are reductionary (p. 21). Predetermined methods that map out an order to be followed toward closure betray differences offered through ongoing attention toward otherness. Curricular conversations are then apt to be monolithic and, thus, uncomplicated. Davey explains: "the will to method has an impervious insensitivity to other voices and reduces the complex variety of human experience to its own terms" (p. 21). Complicated curricular conversations confront the risks and opportunities of exposing other voices and diversities. Aesthetic play's commitment to openness continually invests in keeping the movement of thinking moving.

Finally, Davey (2006) describes how the will to method promotes a dehumanizing mode of consciousness (p. 22). He explains that blindness to self-understandings to be gained through exposure to differences limits what is encountered and ethically constrains what is then understood. At an extreme, the potential for a dehumanizing form of consciousness separates self from situations operating in a mechanical mode that does not question, scrutinize, analyze, discern, reflect, speculate, adapt, change, or build meaning. It is preoccupation with the will to method that Davey claims "masks a failure (or a fear) to confront the risks of what it is to be merely human" (p. 22). The questioning, scrutinizing, analyzing, discerning, reflecting, speculating, adapting, changing, and building self attends to these risks. The chapters that comprise this book attend to the intricacies encountered as the "unquiet" understandings evoked through aesthetic play, shaping learning and learners.

"Unquiet understanding," as Davey (2006) maps out, asks all involved to resist residing in the quiet of a single interpretation (p. xvi). Aesthetic play's insistence on the participatory terms of engagement, valuing the formative terrain of all sense-making, expects openness to the unquiet understandings disclosed en-route. Each chapter of this book reflects the unquiet lived terms as the matters that ought to matter within sense-making of all kinds. Aesthetic play, as a force of the possible, navigates the necessary movement for new and enlarged ways to see and engage the world. Aesthetic play—as elemental to being human—insists upon inherent curiosities, suggestions, and found order as holding the resources for learning. Aesthetic play—as embracing of place—values, respects, and converses with the particulars inhering place. Aesthetic play—as needing other(s)—fosters understandings of self that are constituted and reconstituted always in relation to other(s). Aesthetic play—as spatial/temporal negotiation—demands mindfulness of present circumstances alongside speculative sensibilities. Aesthetic play—as interdependent with imagination, instilling embodied understandings—coheres a lived unity of sense that comprehends through the entire body. Aesthetic play—as attunement to process—fosters trust in the contingent ground of meaning-making itself. Aesthetic play—as acquiring self-understandings in relation to wider contexts and citizenry—expands personal and collective horizons. The role of unquiet understandings as catalytic to self-formation surfaces as my self-narrative enters into the play each artwork affords me. The reader brings their own understandings into play and as Gallagher (1992) states, "The 'self' involved in play is not a totalized self-identical essence, but ... a self-process which never stops being a process in play" (p. 51). It is through each of these chapters that Gadamer's (2000) transformation into structure gains increasing texture and tangibility. The relational whole is the terrain of aesthetic play, marked by unquiet understandings that denote the contingent ground encountered, and form and inform selves in the making.

Makings of Self/World

Aesthetic play, as Gadamer (2000) contends, is continually restructured by those who play along. As a whole, the book conveys this movement. It is a movement that is infused with Merleau-Ponty's (1964) paradox of *immanence* and *transcendence*. As each artwork draws me into its immanent, pervading workings, the agentic possibilities of transcendence are suggested. Readers are asked to engage similarly. It is the interplay of immanence and transcendence that forms the relational ground for aesthetic play. Immanence entails the sustained attention to qualities at play within each artwork. It is only through such attention that those qualities come to be known. And those qualities increasingly draw my attention to the relationships among them, as each chapter folds into the other. Such qualitative thought requires the willing immersion of self in situation, gaining cognizance of the immanent qualities at play. Eisner (1985) states that it is this "ability to read the qualitative world in which we live" that "is the major avenue through which those forms we call thoughts are constructed" (p. 68). Such readings of the qualitative world are always moving. Each chapter reads the uncertain terrain, navigating the evolving relationships, with meanings transcending its artwork. Curricular possibilities abound and transcend disciplines, interests, and age levels. The paradox of immanence and transcendence forms a nexus of shifting meanings that positions all involved to live within the workings, invigorated by the tensional in-dwelling (Aoki, 1992) of unquiet understandings that surface, thus, seeking, making, deepening, and extending meanings. The fragility and tentativeness of this immanent and transcendent movement holds aesthetic play's strength and vitality. It is this ongoing search, locating self within this movement, that accords aesthetic play primary consideration within education.

Pinar (2011) describes the immanent and transcendent movement at play as the experience of arts "pull(ing) us into the world as it refracts the world through our subjectivity; the educational undertaking involves inhabiting the middle while grounded in, attentive to, and engaged with both self and society" (p. 100). Gadamer (1986) cautions "that it is failure to recognize the universal scope and ontological dignity of play ... that blinds us to the interdependence of both" (p. 130). It is Pinar's (2011) pull and refraction which chapters of the book each afford as invitations to play. In doing so, the interdependency Gadamer (1986) articulates of self in the world is concretely navigated, moving into unfamiliar terrain, outside of self, transcending the limits of self, and returning to self. It is this interdependent pulling and refracting movement that reconstructs and transforms self. For it is only within such movement that we "catch sight of ourselves in a way that is often unexpected or unfamiliar: what we are, what we might be, and what we are about" (Gadamer, 1986, p. 130). My childhood narrative of self one foggy morning knew such movement to be deeply educative. And it is this movement that forms the complicated curricular conversations that are so desperately missing.

Epilogue

The nihilistic, colonizing, and dehumanizing tendencies Davey (2006) cautions as outcomes of the "will to method" are at odds with aesthetic play. Dewey (1902) similarly termed such outcomes "evils," positioning the child versus the curriculum (p. 202). These evils, suggested throughout each chapter of this book, disregard organic connections between self and the world, thus "there is no craving, no need, no demand" or internal motivation, and opportunities for experiencing "self-reasoning powers" and the potentially "thought provoking character" of curriculum are obscured (p. 204). Aesthetic play unmasks the character of complicated curricular conversations. The texture of these conversations manifests through traversing the ground that unfolds. But, it is up to all educators to explore the shapes these complicated curricular conversations can take with their students, elucidating the thought-provoking character within particular contexts and the specifics of content. I can think of no more important aim for education than to give such *imagery outward manifestation* (Dewey, 1934, p. 278). Aesthetic play holds significances we can no longer ignore, dismiss, or fear. It restores life within learning. Indeed, it seems play and seriousness are interwoven within its enactment. Such interweaving provokes curricular content and structure, exposing the fertile ground of aesthetic play, and offering the sustenance the world needs to think together, investing in living well together.

Aesthetic play provides the clues to the workings of human experience and the unquiet discoveries and unfolding processes of self-formation that an education ought to entail. This is the character of complicated curricular conversations that emerges through aesthetic play. Its character opposes the ubiquitous discourses of contemporary culture that insists on certainties and specific answers. Thinkers, turned to throughout this book, claim play importantly provides the practice ground for the re-creation of freedom and fosters forms of our freedom as human beings. The chapters collectively draw attention to the agency to be gained through play. But play can go wrong. So with agency comes responsibility. Attending to aesthetic play asks all involved to vigilantly attend to the ground of what it moves away from, toward, into, and why (Dewey, 1934). Thus, Greene (1988) does not associate such freedom with autonomy and independence, but rather with interdependence. Aesthetic play provides the concrete practice needed to bring together Greene's call for "wide-awakeness" with the "hunger for community," signifying what it means to be free (p. 23). Dewey's (1934) lifelong emphasis on educators' responsibilities to ensure such educative experiences is a primary reason I find much direction and support in his thinking and seek the freedoms play accesses. Of course, the weight of this responsibility is an ever-pressing one, given today's climate that thwarts teacher and student agency. But it is a weight that educators cannot lose sense of, nor set aside as an extra to insert into their curricular practices occasionally. I have to say that over my many years as an educator I have never worked as hard as I have now, to create the necessary conditions, and foster the associated supports, for practicing and prospective educators to experience aesthetic play and the lived curricular consequences of complicated conversations. Many have little recent experience of what this might look and feel like in practice.

Aesthetic play is a necessity to awaken the artistic/meaning-making spirit in each of us. It is my hope that this book awakens readers to play, and to act on the ensuing possibilities, complicating curriculum-making of all kinds. After all, it is only through educators' belief in the worthiness of aesthetic play that greater commitment to its curricular presence and roles will be acted upon. And it is only through aesthetic play's enactment that its educative significances will take life and play on.

NOTES

1 The artist acknowledges that the title and inspiration for this work comes from the poet, Alfred Joyce Kilmer, and his poem "Trees" (1913).

2 The title of the second chapter comes from John Baldacchino's (2009) book, *Education beyond education: Self and the imaginary in Maxine Greene's philosophy*. New York, NY: Peter Lang. Baldacchino draws on the scholarship of Greene to eloquently illuminate learning's power through re-characterizing the imaginary as a "force of the possible" (p.58).

3 The International Quilt Study Center & Museum was founded in 1997 when native Nebraskans, Ardis, and Robert James donated their collection of nearly 1,000 quilts to the University of Nebraska-Lincoln. Their contribution became the centerpiece of what is now the largest publicly held quilt collection in the world. Through private funds from the University of Nebraska Foundation and a lead gift from the James family, the center opened in its new location in 2008. The glass and brick "green" building houses more than 3,500 quilts, as well as state-of-the-art research and storage space, and custom-crafted galleries. The new facility enhances the center's ability to pursue its mission: to collect, preserve, study, exhibit, and promote discovery of quilts and quilt-making traditions from many cultures, countries, and times. The International Quilt Study Center & Museum is an academic program of the Department of Textiles, Clothing and Design in the College of Education and Human Sciences at UNL. The department offers a unique masters degree in Textile History with a quilt studies emphasis, which is the only program of its kind in the world. See www.Quilt-Study.org for more information.

4 The Sheldon Museum of Art houses both the Sheldon Art Association collection founded in 1888, and the University of Nebraska collection, initiated in 1929. Together they comprise more than 12,000 works of art in all media. This comprehensive collection of American art includes prominent holdings of 19th-century landscape and still life, American Impressionism, early Modernism, geometric abstraction, Abstract Expressionism, pop, minimalism and contemporary art. In the Sculpture Garden more than 30 monumental sculptures are exhibited year-round and include major works by Gaston Lachaise, Jacques Lipchitz, Claes Oldenburg and Coosje van Bruggen, David Smith, William Tucker, Bryan Hunt, Mark di Suvero, Michael Heizer, and Richard Serra. The Stuart P. Embury American Art Research Library will

complement the existing research library with more than 10,000 volumes document-ing the history of American art. The Sheldon's exhibition program comprises approxi-mately 20 exhibitions per year and focuses on American art in all media. The curatorial staff organizes exhibitions drawn from the permanent collection, many of which circulate nationally. The program also includes exhibitions organized by peer institu-tions throughout the United States. Educational programs such as symposia, lectures, children's workshops and tours are organized in conjunction with each exhibition. The Sheldon Museum of Art is located at 12 & R Streets in Lincoln, NE 68588–0300. For additional information see www.sheldonartmuseum.org.

5 Conversations throughout a graduate-level curriculum theory class in the Department of Teaching, Learning, and Teacher Education at the University of Nebraska-Lincoln in the spring of 2008 formed the development of this chapter. I am thankful for the educators in this course who contributed to the rich substance of these conversations.

6 See note 4 regarding the Sheldon Museum of Art at the University of Nebraska-Lincoln: www.sheldonartmuseum.org.

7 I am indebted to Phuong, Anthony, and Uyen for their willingness to share their per-spectives and insights with me to enable the development of this chapter.

BIBLIOGRAPHY

Abrams, D. (1996). *The spell of the sensuous: Perception and language in a more than human world*. New York: Pantheon Books.

Alexander, T. M. (1998). The art of life: Dewey's aesthetics. In L. A. Hickman (Ed.), *Dewey: Interpretations for a postmodern generation* (pp. 1–22). Bloomington, IN: Indiana University Press.

Alexander, T. M. (2003). Between being and emptiness: Toward an eco-ontology of inhabitation. In W. J. Gavin (Ed.), *In Dewey's wake: Unfinished work of pragmatic reconstruction* (pp. 129–158). Albany, NY: State University of New York Press.

Anttila, E. (2007). Children as agents in dance: Implications of the notion of child culture for research and practice in dance education. In L. Bresler (Ed.), *International handbook of research in arts education* (pp. 865–879). Dordrecht: Springer.

Aoki, T. T. (1992). Layered voices of teaching: The uncannily correct and the elusively true. In W. F. Pinar & W. M. Reynolds (Eds.), *Understanding curriculum as phenomenological and deconstructed text* (pp. 25–26). New York, NY: Teachers College Press.

Arendt, H. (1958). *The human condition*. Chicago, IL: University of Chicago Press.

Aristotle (1925). *The nicomachean ethics* (D. Ross, Trans). Oxford: Oxford University Press.

Bakhtin, M. M. (1919 [1990]). *Art and answerability: Early philosophical essays*. Austin, TX: University of Texas Press.

Bakhtin, M. M. (1984). *Problems of Dostoevsky's poetics* (Ed. and Trans. Caryl Emerson). Minneapolis, MN: University of Michigan Press.

Bakhtin, M. M. (1993). *Toward a philosophy of the act*. Austin, TX: University of Texas Press.

Bal, M. (2002). *Travelling concepts in the humanities: A rough guide*. Toronto: University of Toronto Press.

Baldacchino, J. (2009). *Education beyond education: Self and the imaginary in Maxine Greene's philosophy*. New York, NY: Peter Lang.

Barone, T. (1983). Education as aesthetic experience: Art in germ. *Educational Leadership*, *40*(4), 21–26.

Barone, T. (2001). *Touching eternity: The enduring outcomes of teaching*. New York, NY: Teachers College Press.

Berger, J. (1972). *Ways of seeing*. New York, NY: Penguin Books.

Biesta, G. (2004). Mind the gap! In C. Bingham & A. Sidorkin (Eds.), *No education without relation* (pp. 11–22). New York, NY: Peter Lang.

Biesta, G. (2007). Why "what works" won't work: Evidence-based practice and the democratic deficit of educational research. *Educational Theory 57*(1), 1–22.

Bingham, C., & Sidorkin, A. M. (Eds.). (2004). *No education without relation*. New York, NY: Peter Lang.

Block, A. A. (2001). *I'm only bleeding: Education as the practice of social violence against children*. New York, NY: Peter Lang.

Blumenfeld-Jones, D. (1995). Curriculum, control, and creativity. *Journal of Curriculum Theorizing, 11*(1), 73–96.

Boisvert, R. D. (1998). *John Dewey: Rethinking our times*. New York, NY: SUNY Press.

Borko, H. (2004). Professional development and teacher learning: Mapping the terrain. *Educational Researcher, 33*(8), 3–15.

Bourriaud, N. (1998). *Relational aesthetics*. France: Les Presses du Réel.

Bowman, W. (2004). Cognition and the body: Perspectives from music education. In L. Bresler (Ed.), *Knowing bodies, moving minds: Towards embodied teaching and learning* (pp. 29–50). Boston, MA: Kluwer.

Bresler, L. (Ed.). (2004). *Knowing bodies, moving minds: Towards embodied teaching and learning*. Dordrecht/Boston, MA/London: Kluwer.

Britzman, D. (1991). *Practice makes practice*. New York, NY: SUNY Press.

Brookfield, S. (1995). *Becoming a critically reflective teacher*. San Francisco, CA: Jossey-Bass.

Bruner, J. (1990). *Acts of meaning*. Cambridge, MA: Harvard University Press.

Bullough, R. V., Jr., & Baughman, K. (1997). *First year teachers eight years later: An inquiry into teacher development*. New York, NY: Teachers College Press.

Cain, P. (2010). *Drawing: The enactive evolution of the practitioner*. Bristol: Intellect.

Cain, P. (2011). Drawings (on) Riverside Exhibition. Retrieved November 20, 2011, from www.patriciacain.com/index.html.

Castle, J. B. (1997). Toward understanding professional development: Exploring views across a professional development school. *Teachers and Teaching: Theory and Practice, 3*(2), 221–242.

Chambers, C. (2006). The land is the best teacher I ever had: Places as pedagogy for precarious times. *Journal of Curriculum Theorizing, 22*(3), 27–37.

Chambers, C. (2008). Where are we? Finding common ground in a curriculum of place. *Journal of the Canadian Association for Curriculum Studies, 6*(2), 113–128.

Chappell, D. (Ed.). (2010). *Children under construction: Critical essays on play as curriculum*. New York, NY: Peter Lang.

Cochran-Smith, M. (2001). Constructing outcomes in teacher education: Policy, practice and pitfalls. *Education Policy Analysis Archives, 9*(11), 1–57.

Cochran-Smith, M. (2003). The unforgiving complexity of teaching: Avoiding simplicity in the age of accountability. *Journal of Teacher Education, 54*(1), 3–5.

Cochran-Smith, M., Feiman-Nemser, S., McIntyre, D. J., & Demers, K. E. (2008). (Eds.), *Handbook of research on teacher education*. New York, NY: Routledge.

Cochran-Smith, M., & Lytle, S. L. (2009). *Inquiry as stance: Practitioner research for the next generation*. New York, NY: Teachers College Press.

Crowther, P. (1993). *Art and embodiment*. Oxford: Clarendon Press.

Csordes, T. J. (1994). *Embodiment and experience*. Cambridge: Cambridge University Press.

Danh, B. (2011). Projects. Retrieved September 6, 2011, from http://binhdanh.com/projects.html.

Darling-Hammond, L. (1996). The quiet revolution: Rethinking teacher development. *Educational Leadership, 53*(6), 4–10.

Darling-Hammond, L. (2006). Securing the right to learn: Policy and practice for powerful teaching and learning. *Educational Researcher, 35*(7), 13–24.

Davey, N. (2006). *Unquiet understanding: Gadamer's philosophical hermeneutics*. New York, NY: State University of New York Press.

Day, C. (2000). Stories of change and professional development: The costs of commitment. In C. Day, A. Fernandez, T. Hauge, & J. Moller (Eds.), *The life and work of teachers: International perspectives in changing times* (pp. 109–129). London: Falmer.

Day, C. (2004). *A passion for teaching*. London: Routledge.

Dewey, J. (1902 [1990]). *The child and the curriculum*. Chicago, IL: University of Chicago Press.

Dewey, J. (1904) The relation of theory and practice in education. In C. A. McMurry (Ed.), *The relation of theory to practice in the education of teachers: The third yearbook of the National Society for the Scientific Study of Education*. Chicago, IL: University of Chicago Press.

Dewey, J. (1906 [1977]. Essays on the new empiricism, 1903–1906. In J. A. Boydston (Ed.), *The middle works of John Dewey (Vol. 3)*. Carbondale, IL: Southern Illinois University Press.

Dewey, J. (1910 [1997]). *How we think*. New York, NY: Dover.

Dewey, J. (1916 [1944]). *Democracy and education*. New York, NY: Free Press.

Dewey, J. (1922). *Human nature and conduct*. New York, NY: Holt.

Dewey, J. (1928). *Preoccupation with the disconnected from body and mind*. First published in the *Bulletin of the New York Academy of Medicine*. Body and Mind is included with *The collected works of John Dewey: Later works Vol. 3: 1927–1928*. Carbondale, IL: Southern Illinois University Press.

Dewey, J. (1929). *The quest for certainty*. New York, NY: Putnam.

Dewey, J. (1934). *Art as experience*. New York, NY: Capricorn Books.

Dewey, J. (1938). *Experience and education*. New York, NY: Touchstone.

Dewey, J. (1943 [1990]). *The school and society*. Chicago, IL: University of Chicago Press.

Dewey, J. (1958). *Experience and nature*. New York, NY: Dover.

Dewey, J. (1972). *The early works of John Dewey, 1882–1898 (Vol. 5): Early essays, the early works* (Ed. by J. Boydston). Carbondale, IL: Southern Illinois University Press.

Dissanayake, E. (2000). *Art and intimacy: How the arts began*. Seattle, WA: University of Washington Press.

Doll, W. (2009). The four R's: An alternative to the Tyler rationale. In D. J. Flinders & S. J. Thornton (Eds.), *The curriculum studies reader* (3rd. ed., pp. 348–361). New York, NY: Routledge.

Duckworth, E. (2006). *The having of wonderful ideas and other essays on teaching and learning*. New York, NY: Teachers College Press.

Dunne, J., & Hogan, P. (2004). *Education and practice: Upholding the integrity of teaching and learning*. Malden, MA: Blackwell.

Edwards, C., Gandini, L., & Forman, G. (Eds.). (2011). *The hundred languages of children: The Reggio Emilia experience in transformation*. Santa Barbara, CA: Praeger.

Egan, K. (1992). *Imagination in teaching and learning: The middle school years.* Chicago, IL: University of Chicago Press.

Eisner, E. W. (1972). *Educating artistic vision.* New York, NY: Macmillan.

Eisner, E. W. (1985). *Why art in education and why art education: Beyond creating—the place for art in American schools.* Los Angeles, CA: J. Paul Getty Trust.

Eisner, E. W. (1998). *The enlightened eye: Qualitative inquiry and the enhancement of educational practice.* Upper Saddle River, NJ: Prentice Hall.

Eisner, E. W. (2002). *The arts and the creation of mind.* London: Yale University Press.

Feiman-Nemser, S. (2008). Teacher learning: How do teachers learn to teach? In M. Cochran-Smith, S. Feiman-Nemser, D. J. McIntyre, & K. E. Demers (Eds.), *Handbook of research on teacher education* (pp. 697–705). New York, NY: Routledge.

Freud, S. (1940). The interpretation of dreams (2nd part). In J. Strachey (Ed.), *The standard edition of the complete psychological works of Sigmund Freud* (pp. 339–685). London: Hogarth & Institute for Psychoanalysis.

Frost, J. L. (2010). *A history of children's play and play environments: Toward a contemporary child-saving movement.* New York, NY: Routledge.

Fullan, M. (2007). *The new meaning of educational change* (4th ed.). New York, NY: Teachers College Press.

Gadamer, H. G. (1986). *The relevance of the beautiful and other essays.* Cambridge: Cambridge University Press.

Gadamer, H. (2000). *Truth and method.* New York, NY: Continuum.

Gallagher, S. (1992). *Hermeneutics and education.* New York, NY: State University of New York Press.

Gallego, M. A., Hollingsworth, S., & Whitenack, D. A. (2001). Relational knowing in the reform of educational cultures. *Teachers College Record, 2,* 240–266.

Garet, M., Birman, B., Porter, A., Desimone, L., & Suk Yoon, K. (2001). What makes professional development effective? Results from a national sample of teachers. *American Educational Research Journal, 38*(4), 915–945.

Garrison, J. (1997). *Dewey and eros: Wisdom and desire in the art of teaching.* New York, NY: Teachers College Press.

Garrison, J., & Rud, A. (2009) Reverence in classroom teaching. *Teachers College Record, 111*(11), 2626–2646.

Gaudelli, W., & Hewitt, R. (2010). The aesthetic potential of global issues curriculum. *Journal of Aesthetic Education, 44*(2), 83–99.

Goldsworthy, A. (2004) *Rivers and tides: Working with time* [DVD]. Directed by Thomas Riedelsheimer. Mediopolis Films.

Granger, D. A. (2003). Expression, imagination, and organic unity: John Dewey's aesthetics and romanticism. *Journal of Aesthetic Education, 37*(2), 46–60.

Granger, D. A. (2006). *John Dewey, Robert Persig, and the art of living: Revisioning aesthetic education.* New York, NY: Palgrave Macmillan.

Green, B., & Reid, J. (2008). Method(s) in our madness? Poststructuralism, pedagogy and teacher education. In A. Phelan & J. Sumsion (Eds.), *Critical readings in teacher education: Provoking absences* (pp. 17–31). Rotterdam: Sense.

Greene, M. (1988). *The dialectic of freedom.* New York, NY: Teachers College Press.

Greene, M. (1995). *Releasing the imagination: Essays on education, the arts, and social change.* San Francisco, CA: Jossey-Bass.

Greene, M. (2001). *Variations on a blue guitar: The Lincoln Center Institute lectures on aesthetic education.* New York, NY: Teachers College Press.

Griffiths, V. (2000). The reflective dimension in teacher education. *International Journal of Educational Research, 33*(5), 539–555.

Grosz, F. (1994). *Volatile bodies.* Bloomington, IN: Indiana University Press.

Groundwater-Smith, S., & Mockler, N. (2009). *Teacher professional learning in an age of compliance: Mind the gap.* London: Springer.

Grumet, M. R. (1988). *Bitter milk: Women and teaching.* Boston, MA: University of Massachusetts Press.

Grumet, M. R. (2006). Where does the world go when schooling is about schooling? *Journal of Curriculum Theorizing, 22*(3), 47–54.

Hanna, J. L. (2008). A nonverbal language for imagining and learning: Dance education in K-12 curriculum. *Educational Researcher, 37*(8), 491–506.

Hansen, D. T. (2005). Creativity in teaching and building a meaningful life as a teacher. *Journal of Aesthetic Education, 39*(2), 57–68.

Hansen, D. T. (2011). *The teacher and the world: A study of cosmopolitanism as education.* New York, NY: Routledge.

Hargreaves, A. (2002). Teaching in a box: Emotional geographies of teaching. In C. Sugrue & C. Day (Eds.), *Developing teachers and teaching practice: International research perspectives* (pp. 3–25). London: Routledge Falmer.

Hargreaves, A., & Shirley, D. (2009). The persistence of presentism. *Teachers College Record, 111*(11), 2505–2534.

Hegel, G. W. (1835 [1964]). The philosophy of fine art. In S. Hofstadter & R. Kuhns (Eds.), *Philosophies of art and beauty* (pp. 382–445). Chicago, IL: University of Chicago Press.

Hostetler, K. (2011). *Seducing souls: Education and the experience of human well-being.* New York, NY: Continuum.

Hostetler, K., Macintyre Latta, M., & Sarroub, L. (2007). Retrieving meaning in teacher education: The question of meaning. *Journal of Teacher Education, 58*(3), 231–244.

Hunsberger, M. (1992). The time of texts. In W. F. Pinar & W. M. Reynolds (Eds.), *Understanding curriculum as phenomenological and deconstructed text* (pp. 64–91). New York, NY: Teachers College Press.

Irwin, R. L., & de Cosson, A. (Eds.). (2004). *a/r/tography: Rendering self through arts-based living inquiry.* Vancouver: Pacific Educational.

Jackson, P. (1998). *John Dewey and the lessons of art.* Boston, MA: Yale University Press.

Jackson, P. (2001). John Dewey's 1906 definition of art. *Teachers College Record.* Retrieved on June 14, 2002, from www.tcrecord.org, ID Number: 10736.

Jardine, D. W. (1992). Reflections on education, hermeneutics, and ambiguity: Hermeneutics as a restoring of life to its original difficulty. In W. F. Pinar & W. M. Reynolds (Eds.), *Understanding curriculum as phenomenological and deconstructed text* (pp. 116–127). New York, NY: Teachers College Press.

Johnson, M. (2007). *The meaning of the body: Aesthetics of human understanding.* Chicago, IL: University of Chicago Press.

Kant, I. (1790 [1952]). *The critique of judgment.* Oxford: Clarendon.

Kemmis, S., & Smith, T. J. (2008). *Enabling praxis: Challenges for educators.* Rotterdam: Sense.

Kennedy, S. (2008). *Agency of time: An installation by Leighton Pierce, Interview with artist.* Retrieved March 15, 2011, from www.sheldonartmuseum.org/exhibitions.

Kerdeman, D. (2003). Pulled up short: Challenging self-understanding as a focus of teaching and learning. *Journal of Philosophy of Education, 37*(2), 293–308.

Korsmeyer, C. (Ed.). (1998). *Aesthetics: The big questions*. New York, NY: Wiley.

Korthagen, F. (2001). *Linking practice and theory: The pedagogy of realistic teacher education*. Mahwah, NJ: Lawrence Erlbaum.

Korthagen, F., & Vasalos, A. (2005). Levels in reflection: Core reflection as a means to enhance professional growth. *Teachers and Teaching: Theory and Practice, 11*(1), 47–71.

Kwok-bun, C. (2005). *Chinese identities, ethnicity and cosmoploitanism*. London: Routledge.

Laberee, D. (2000). On the nature of teaching and teacher education: Difficult practices that look easy. *Journal of Teacher Education, 51*(3), 228–233.

Loughran, J. (2006). *Developing a pedagogy of teacher education: Understanding teaching and learning about teaching*. New York, NY: Routledge.

Loughran, J. (2010). *What expert teachers do: Enhancing professional knowledge for classroom practice*. New York, NY: Routledge.

MacIntyre, A. (1999). *Dependent rational animals: Why human beings need the virtues*. Chicago, IL: Open Court.

Macintyre Latta, M. (2001). *The possibilities of play in the classroom: On the power of aesthetic experience in teaching, learning, and researching*. New York, NY: Peter Lang.

Macintyre Latta, M. (2004). Confronting a forgetfulness and deformation of teaching/learning methodology. *Teachers & Teaching: Theory and Practice, 10*(3), 329–344.

Macintyre Latta, M. (2005). The role and place of fear in what it means to teach and to learn. *Teaching Education, 16*(3), 183–196.

Macintyre Latta, M., & Baer, S. (2010). Aesthetic inquiry: About, within, without, and through repeated visits. In T. Costantino & B. White (Eds.), *Essays on aesthetic education for the 21st century* (pp. 93–108). Rotterdam: Sense.

Macintyre Latta, M., Buck, G., Leslie-Pelecky, D., & Carpenter, L. (2007). Terms of inquiry. *Teachers & Teaching: Theory and Practice, 13*(1), 21–41.

Macintyre Latta, M., & Chan, E. (2011). *Teaching the arts to engage English language learners*. New York, NY: Routledge.

Macintyre Latta, M., & Wunder, S. (2012). Investing in the formative nature of professional learning: Redirecting, mediating, and generating education practice-as-policy. In M. Macintyre Latta & S. Wunder (Eds.), *Placing practitioner knowledge at the center of teacher education: Rethinking the policies and practices of the education doctorate*. Charlotte, NC: Information Age.

McLaren, N., & Lambert, E. (1949). *Begone dull care*. Canadian National Film Board.

May, W. (1993). Teaching as a work of art in the medium of curriculum. *Theory into Practice, 32*(4), 210–218.

Meier, D., Engel, B. S., & Taylor, B. (2010). *Playing for keeps: Life and learning on a public school playground*. New York, NY: Teachers College Press.

Merleau-Ponty, M. (1962). *The phenomenology of perception*. Evanston, IL: Northwestern University Press.

Merleau-Ponty, M. (1964). *The primacy of perception*. Evanston, IL: Northwestern University Press.

Merleau-Ponty, M. (1968). *The visible and the invisible* (Trans. Alphonso Lingis). Evanston, IL: Northwestern University Press.

Mockler, N., & Groundwater-Smith, S. (2009). From lesson-study to learning study: Side-by-side professional learning in the classroom. In A. Campbell & S. Groundwater-Smith (Eds.), *Connecting inquiry and professional learning in education: Joining the dots*. Abingdon: Routledge.

Morgan, S. (2011). Anything I can stick a needle in: An interview with Yvonne Wells. *Journal of Comparative Poetics, 31*, 63–94.

Munby, M., Russell, T., & Martin, A. K. (2001). Teachers' knowledge and how it develops. In V. Richarson (Ed.), *Handbook of research on teaching* (4th ed., pp. 877–904). Washington, DC: American Educational Research Association.

Napoli, J. (2011). Floodwall. Retrieved August 14, 2011, from www.floodwall.org.

National Council for Accreditation of Teacher Education. (2010). *Transforming teacher education through clinical practice: A national strategy to prepare effective teachers*. Washington, DC: National Council for Accreditation of Teacher Education.

National Law Center for Homelessness and Poverty. (2005). National policy and advocacy council on homelessness report. Retrieved January 8, 2011, from www.npach. org.

Nias, J. (1996). Thinking about feeling: The emotions in teaching. *Journal of Education, 26*(3), 293–306.

Noddings, N. (1984). *Caring: A feminine approach to ethics and moral education*. Berkeley, CA: University of California Press.

Noddings, N. (1993). *Educating for intelligent belief or unbelief*. New York, NY: Teachers College Press.

Noddings, N. (1996). Stories and affect in teacher education. *Journal of Education, 26*(3), 435–447.

Nussbaum, M. C. (2010). *Not for profit: Why democracy needs the humanities*. Princeton, NJ: Princeton University Press.

O'Loughlin, M. (1995). Intelligent bodies and ecological subjectivities: Merleau-Ponty's corrective to postmodernism's "subjects" of education. In A. Neiman (Ed.), *Philosophy of education yearbook* (pp. 334–342). Urbana, IL: University of Illinois at Urbana-Champaign.

O'Loughlin, M. (2006). *Embodiment and education: Exploring creatural existence*. Dordrecht: Springer.

Paley, V. G. (2004). *A child's work: The importance of fantasy play*. Chicago, IL: University of Chicago Press.

Palmer, P. (1998). *The courage to teach*. San Francisco, CA: Jossey-Bass.

Phelan, A., & Sumsion, J. (Eds.). (2008). *Critical readings in teacher education: Provoking absences*. Rotterdam: Sense.

Pierce, L. (2008). Leighton Pierce. Retreived October 1, 2011, from www.leighton-pierce.com.

Pinar, W. F. (Ed.). (2003). *International handbook of curriculum research*. Mahwah, NJ: Lawrence Erlbaum.

Pinar, W. F. (2009) *The worldliness of a cosmopolitan education: Passionate lives in public education*. New York, NY: Routledge.

Pinar, W. F. (2010). Notes on a blue guitar. *Journal of Educational Controversy, 5*(1). Retrieved on March 1, 2010, from www.wce.wwu.edu/Resources/CEP/eJournal/v005n001/a004.shtml.

Pinar, W. F. (2011). *The character of curriculum studies: Bildung, currere, and the recurring question of the subject*. New York, NY: Palgrave Macmillan.

Pinar, W., Reynolds, W. M., Slattery, P., & Taubman, P. M. (1995) *Understanding curriculum*. New York, NY: Peter Lang.

Pipher, M. (2002). *The middle of everywhere: The world's refugees come to our town*. Orlando, FL: Harcourt.

Raikes, H. (2011). *Corpus corvus.* Retrieved December 18, 2011, from www.heather-raikes.com/corpus-corvus-2011.

Richard, V. T. (1982). *Norman McLaren, manipulator of movement: The national film board years, 1947–1967.* Toronto: University of Delaware Press.

Richmond, S., & Snowber, C. (2009). *Landscapes of aesthetic education.* Newcastle upon Tyne: Cambridge Scholars.

Risser, J. (1997). *Hermeneutics and the voice of the other: Re-reading Gadamer's philosophica hermeneutics.* New York, NY: State University of New York Press.

Russell, D. (1998). Cultivating the imagination in music education: John Dewey's theory of imagination and its relation to the Chicago laboratory school. *Educational Theory, 48*(2), 193–210.

Schiller, F. (1795 [1954]). *On the aesthetic education of man in a series of letters.* New York, NY: Frederick Unger.

Schon, D. (1987). *Educating the reflective practitioner.* San Francisco, CA: Jossey-Bass.

Schon, D. (1995). The new scholarship requires a new epistemology. *Change: The Magazine of Higher Learning, 27*(6), 27–34.

Schuck, S., & Russell, T. (2005). Self-study, critical friendship, and the complexities of teacher education. *Studying Teacher Education, 3*(2), 107–121.

Schwab, J. J. (1976). Education and the state: Learning community. In R. M. Hutchins & M. J. Adler (Eds.), *The great ideas today, 1976* (pp. 234–271). Chicago, IL: Encyclopedia Britannica.

Shakespeare, W. (1922). *Shakespeare's Hamlet, Prince of Denmark.* New York, NY: E.P. Dutton.

Sidorkin, A. (2002). *Relational pedagogy.* New York, NY: Peter Lang.

Siegesmund, R. (2010). Aesthetics as a curriculum of care and responsible choice. In T. Costantino & B. White (Eds.), *Essays on aesthetic education for the 21st century* (pp. 81–92). Rotterdam: Sense.

Simpson, D. J., Jackson, M. B., & Aycock, J. C. (2005). *John Dewey and the art of teaching: Toward reflective and imaginative practice.* Thousand Oaks, CA: Sage.

Singer, D. G., Michnick Golinkoff, R., & Hirsh-Pasek (Eds.). (2006). *Play = learning: How play motivates and enhances children's cognitive and social emotional growth.* New York, NY: Oxford University Press.

Smith, D. (1996). Identity, self, and other in the conduct of pedagogical action: An East/West inquiry. *Journal of Curriculum Theorizing, 12*(3), 6–12.

Smith, D. (2006). *Trying to teach in a season of great untruth: Globalization, empire and the crises of pedagogy.* Rotterdam: Sense.

Snowber, C. N. (2007). The soul moves: Dance and spirituality in educative practice. In L. Bresler (Ed.), *International handbook of research in arts education* (pp. 1449–1456). Dordrecht: Springer.

Taubman, P. M. (2009). *Teaching by numbers: Deconstructing the discourse of standards and accountability in education.* New York, NY: Routledge.

Taubman, P. M. (2012). Disavowed knowledge: Psychoanalysis, education, and teaching. New York, NY: Routledge.

Thayer-Bacon, B. J. (2004). Personal and social relations in education. In C. Bingham & A. M. Sidorkin (Eds.), *No education without relation* (pp. 165–179). New York, NY: Peter Lang.

Thompson, C. M. (2007). The culture of childhood and the visual arts. In L. Bresler (Ed.), *International handbook of research in arts education* (pp. 899–913). Dordrecht: Springer.

Thornton, S. J. (2005). *Teaching social studies that matters: Curriculum for active learning.* New York, NY: Teachers College Press.

Van Manen, M. (1991). *The tact of teaching.* Albany, NY: SUNY.

Varela, F. (1986). Laying down a path in walking: A biologist's look at a new biology. *Cybernetic, 2,* 6–15.

Varela, F. (1995). The emergent self. In J. Brockman (Ed.), *The third culture beyond the scientific revolution.* New York, NY: Simon & Schuster.

Varela, F. (1997). Patterns of life: Intertwining identity and cognition. *Brain Cognition, 34,* 72–87.

Waks, L. J. (2009). Inquiry, agency, and art: John Dewey's contribution to pragmatic cosmopolitanism. *Education and Culture, 25*(2), 115–125.

Warren Little, J. (2002). Locating learning in teachers' communities of practice: Opening up problems of analysis in records of everyday work. *Teaching and Teacher Education, 18,* 917–946.

Wells, Y. (2012). Storytelling in the gallery, artist talk, November 11, Quilted Messages, International Quilt Study Center & Museum, Lois Gottsch Gallery, University of Nebraska-Lincoln, Lincoln, NE, USA.

Williamson McDiarmid, G., & Clevenger-Bright, M. (2008). Rethinking teacher capacity. In M. Cochran-Smith, S. Feiman-Nemser, & D. J. McIntyre (Eds.), *Handbook of research on teacher education: Enduring questions in changing contexts* (pp. 134–156). New York, NY: Routledge.

Winston, J. (2010). *Beauty and education.* New York, NY: Routledge.

Yinger, R. J. (1988). Community and place in the conversation of teaching. Paper presented at the Florida Conference on Reflective Inquiry: Contexts and Assessments, Orlando, Florida, October 20–22.

Zeichner, K. M., & Liston, D. P. (1996). *Reflective teaching: An introduction.* Mahwah, NJ: Lawrence Erlbaum.

INDEX

Page numbers in **bold** denote figures.